# THE ARGONAUTS OF
# NORTH LIBERTY

## BRET HARTE

1st WORLD
LIBRARY
Literary Society

# The Argonauts of North Liberty

Bret Harte

© 1st World Library, 2007
PO Box 2211
Fairfield, IA 52556
www.1stworldlibrary.com
First Edition

LCCN: 2007930724

Softcover ISBN: 978-1-4218-4800-6
Hardcover ISBN: 978-1-4218-4703-0
eBook ISBN: 978-1-4218-4897-6

Purchase *"The Argonauts of North Liberty"*
as a traditional bound book at:
www.1stWorldLibrary.com/purchase.asp?ISBN=978-1-4218-4800-6

1st World Library is a literary, educational organization
dedicated to:

- Creating a free internet library of downloadable ebooks

- Hosting writing competitions and offering book publishing
  scholarships.

Interested in more 1st World Library books? contact:
literacy@1stworldlibrary.com
Check us out at: www.1stworldlibrary.com

# 1$^{st}$ World Library Literary Society

## Giving Back to the World

"If you want to work on the core problem, it's early school literacy."

**- James Barksdale, former CEO of Netscape**

"No skill is more crucial to the future of a child, or to a democratic and prosperous society, than literacy."

**- Los Angeles Times**

"Literacy... means far more than learning how to read and write... The aim is to transmit... knowledge and promote social participation."

**- UNESCO**

"Literacy is not a luxury, it is a right and a responsibility. If our world is to meet the challenges of the twenty-first century we must harness the energy and creativity of all our citizens."

**- President Bill Clinton**

"Parents should be encouraged to read to their children, and teachers should be equipped with all available techniques for teaching literacy, so the varying needs and capacities of individual kids can be taken into account."

**- Hugh Mackay**

# PART I

## CHAPTER I

The bell of the North Liberty Second Presbyterian Church had just ceased ringing. North Liberty, Connecticut, never on any day a cheerful town, was always bleaker and more cheerless on the seventh, when the Sabbath sun, after vainly trying to coax a smile of reciprocal kindliness from the drawn curtains and half-closed shutters of the austere dwellings and the equally sealed and hard-set churchgoing faces of the people, at last settled down into a blank stare of stony astonishment. On this chilly March evening of the year 1850, that stare had kindled into an offended sunset and an angry night that furiously spat sleet and hail in the faces of the worshippers, and made them fight their way to the church, step by step, with bent heads and fiercely compressed lips, until they seemed to be carrying its forbidding portals at the point of their umbrellas.

Within that sacred but graceless edifice, the rigors of the hour and occasion reached their climax. The shivering gasjets lit up the austere pallor of the bare walls, and the hollow, shell-like sweep of colorless vacuity behind the cold communion table. The chill of despair and hopeless renunciation was in the air, untempered by any glow from the sealed air-tight stove that seemed only to bring out a lukewarm exhalation of wet clothes and cheaply dyed umbrellas. Nor did the presence of the worshippers themselves impart any life to the dreary apartment. Scattered throughout the white pews, in dull, shapeless, neutral blotches, rigidly separated from each other, they seemed only to accent the colorless church and the emptiness of all things. A few children, who had huddled together for warmth in one of the back benches and who had became glutinous and adherent through moisture, were laboriously drawn out and painfully picked apart by a watchful deacon.

The dry, monotonous disturbance of the bell had given way to the strain of a bass viol, that had been apparently pitched to the key of the east wind without, and the crude complaint of a new harmonium that seemed to bewail its limited prospect of ever becoming seasoned or mellowed in its earthly tabernacle, and then the singing began. Here and there a human voice soared and struggled above the narrow text and the monotonous cadence with a cry of individual longing, but was borne down by the dull, trampling precision of the others' formal chant. This and a certain muffled raking of the stove by the sexton brought the temperature down still lower. A sermon, in keeping with the previous performance, in which the chill east wind of doctrine was not tempered to any shorn lamb within that dreary fold, followed. A spark of human and vulgar interest was momentarily kindled by the collection and the simultaneous movement of reluctant hands towards their owners' pockets; but the coins fell on the baize-covered plates with a dull thud, like clods on a coffin, and the dreariness returned. Then there was another hymn and a prolonged moan from the harmonium, to which mysterious suggestion the congregation rose and began slowly to file into the aisle. For a moment they mingled; there was the silent grasping of damp woollen mittens and cold black gloves, and the whispered interchange of each other's names with the prefix of "Brother" or "Sister," and an utter absence of fraternal geniality, and then the meeting slowly dispersed.

The few who had waited until the minister had resumed his hat, overcoat, and overshoes, and accompanied him to the door, had already passed out; the sexton was turning out the flickering gas jets one by one, when the cold and austere silence was broken by a sound—the unmistakable echo of a kiss of human passion.

As the horror-stricken official turned angrily, the figure of a man glided from the shadow of the stairs below the organ loft, and vanished through the open door. Before the sexton could follow, the figure of a woman slipped out of the same portal and with a hurried glance after the first retreating figure, turned in the opposite direction and was lost in the darkness. By the time the indignant and scandalized custodian had reached the portal, they had both melted in the troubled sea of tossing umbrellas already to the right and left of him, and pursuit and recognition were hopeless.

# CHAPTER II

The male figure, however, after mingling with his fellow-worshippers to the corner of the block, stopped a moment under the lamp-post as if uncertain as to the turning, but really to cast a long, scrutinizing look towards the scattered umbrellas now almost lost in the opposite direction. He was still gazing and apparently hesitating whether to retrace his steps, when a horse and buggy rapidly driven down the side street passed him. In a brief glance he evidently recognized the driver, and stepping over the curbstone called in a brief authoritative voice:

"Ned!"

The occupant of the vehicle pulled up suddenly, leaned from the buggy, and said in an astonished tone:

"Dick Demorest! Well! I declare! hold on, and I'll drive up to the curb."

"No; stay where you are."

The speaker approached the buggy, jumped in beside the occupant, refastened the apron, and coolly taking the reins from his companion's hand, started the horse forward. The action was that of an habitually imperious man; and the only

Bret Harte

recognition he made of the other's ownership was the question:

"Where were you going?"

"Home—to see Joan," replied the other. "Just drove over from Warensboro Station. But what on earth are YOU doing here?"

Without answering the question, Demorest turned to his companion with the same good-natured, half humorous authority. "Let your wife wait; take a drive with me. I want to talk to you. She'll be just as glad to see you an hour later, and it's her fault if I can't come home with you now."

"I know it," returned his companion, in a tone of half-annoyed apology. "She still sticks to her old compact when we first married, that she shouldn't be obliged to receive my old worldly friends. And, see here, Dick, I thought I'd talked her out of it as regards YOU at least, but Parson Thomas has been raking up all the old stories about you—you know that affair of the Fall River widow, and that breaking off of Garry Spofferth's match—and about your horse-racing—until—you know, she's more set than ever against knowing you."

"That's not a bad sort of horse you've got there," interrupted Demorest, who usually conducted conversation without reference to alien topics suggested by others. "Where did you get him? He's good yet for a spin down the turnpike and over the bridge. We'll do it, and I'll bring you home safely to Mrs. Blandford inside the hour."

Blandford knew little of horseflesh, but like all men he was not superior to this implied compliment to his knowledge. He resigned himself to his companion as he had been in the habit of doing, and Demorest hurried the horse at a rapid gait down the street until they left the lamps behind, and were fully on the dark turnpike. The sleet rattled against the hood and leathern apron of the buggy, gusts of fierce wind filled the vehicle and seemed to hold it back, but Demorest did not appear to mind it. Blandford thrust his hands deeply into his pockets for warmth, and contracted his shoulders as if in dogged patience. Yet, in spite of the fact that he was tired, cold, and anxious to see his wife, he was conscious of a secret satisfaction in submitting to the caprices of this old friend of his boyhood. After all, Dick Demorest knew what he was about, and had never led him astray by his autocratic will. It was safe to let Dick have his way. It was true it was generally Dick's own way—but he made others think it was theirs too—or would have been theirs had they had the will and the knowledge to project it. He looked up comfortably at the handsome, resolute profile of the man who had taken selfish possession of him. Many women had done the same.

"Suppose if you were to tell your wife I was going to reform," said Demorest, "it might be different, eh? She'd want to take me into the church—'another sinner saved,' and all that, eh?"

"No," said Blandford, earnestly. "Joan isn't as rigid as all that, Dick. What she's got against you is the common report of your free way of living, and that—come now, you know yourself, Dick, that isn't exactly the thing a woman brought up in her style can stand. Why, she thinks I'm unregenerate, and—well, a man can't carry on business always like a class meeting. But are you thinking of reforming?" he continued, trying to get a glimpse of his companion's eyes.

"Perhaps. It depends. Now—there's a woman I know—"

"What, another? and you call this going to reform?" interrupted Blandford, yet not without a certain curiosity in his manner.

"Yes; that's just why I think of reforming. For this one isn't exactly like any other—at least as far as I know."

"That means you don't know anything about her."

"Wait, and I'll tell you." He drew the reins tightly to accelerate the horse's speed, and, half turning to his companion, without, however, moving his eyes from the darkness before him, spoke quickly between the blasts: "I've seen her only half a dozen times. Met her first in 6.40 train out from Boston last fall. She sat next to me. Covered up with wraps and veils; never looked twice at her. She spoke first—kind of half bold, half frightened way. Then got more comfortable and unwound herself, you know, and I saw she was young and not bad-looking. Thought she was some school-girl out for a lark—but rather new at it. Inexperienced, you know, but quite able to take care of herself, by George! and although she looked and acted as if she'd never spoken to a stranger all her life, didn't mind the kind of stuff I talked to her. Rather encouraged it; and laughed—such a pretty little odd laugh, as if laughing wasn't in her usual line, either, and she didn't know how to manage it. Well, it ended in her slipping out at one end of the car when we arrived, while I was looking out for a cab for her at the other." He stopped to recover from a stronger gust of wind. "I—I thought it a good joke on me, and let the thing drop out of my mind, although, mind you, she'd promised to meet me a month afterwards at the same time and place. Well, when the day came I happened to be in Boston, and went to the station. Don't know why I went, for I didn't for a moment think she'd keep her appointment. First, I couldn't find her in the train, but after we'd started she came along out of some seat in the corner, prettier than ever, holding out her hand." He drew a long inspiration. "You can bet your life, Ned, I didn't let go that little hand the rest of the journey."

His passion, or what passed for it, seemed to impart its warmth to the vehicle, and even stirred the chilled pulses of the man beside him.

"Well, who and what was she?"

"Didn't find out; don't know now. For the first thing she made me promise was not to follow her, nor to try to know her name. In return she said she would meet me again on another train near Hartford. She did—and again and again—but always on the train for about an hour, going or coming. Then she missed an appointment. I was regularly cut up, I tell you, and swore as she hadn't kept her word, I wouldn't keep mine, and began to hunt for her. In the midst of it I saw her accidentally; no matter where; I followed her to—well, that's no matter to you, either. Enough that I saw her again—and, well, Ned, such is the influence of that girl over me that, by George! she made me make the same promise again!"

Blandford, a little disappointed at his friend's dogmatic suppression of certain material facts, shrugged his shoulders.

"If that's all your story," he said, "I must say I see no prospect of your reforming. It's the old thing over again, only this time you are evidently the victim. She's some designing creature who will have you if she hasn't already got you completely in her power."

"You don't know what you're talking about, Ned, and you'd better quit," returned Demorest, with cheerful authoritativeness. "I tell you that that's the sort of girl I'm going to marry, if I can, and settle down upon. You can make a memorandum of that, old man, if you like."

Bret Harte

"Then I don't really see why you want to talk to ME about it. And if you are thinking that such a story would go down for a moment with Joan as an evidence of your reformation, you're completely out, Dick. Was that your idea?"

"Yes—and I can tell you, you're wrong again, Ned. You don't know anything about women. You do just as I say—do you understand?—and don't interfere with your own wrong-headed opinions of what other people will think, and I'll take the risks of Mrs. Blandford giving me good advice. Your wife has got a heap more sense on these subjects than you have, you bet. You just tell her that I want to marry the girl and want her to help me—that I mean business, this time—and you'll see how quick she'll come down. That's all I want of you. Will you or won't you?"

With an outward expression of sceptical consideration and an inward suspicion of the peculiar force of this man's dogmatic insight, Blandford assented, with, I fear, the mental reservation of telling the story to his wife in his own way. He was surprised when his friend suddenly drew the horse up sharply, and after a moment's pause began to back him, cramp the wheels of the buggy and then skilfully, in the almost profound darkness, turn the vehicle and horse completely round to the opposite direction.

"Then you are not going over the bridge?" said Blandford.

Demorest made an imperative gesture of silence. The tumultuous rush and roar of swollen and rapid water came from the darkness behind them. "There's been another break-out somewhere, and I reckon the bridge has got all it can do to-night to keep itself out of water without taking us over. At least, as I promised to set you down at your wife's door inside of the hour, I don't propose to try." As the horse now travelled more easily with the wind behind him, Demorest, dismissing abruptly all other subjects, laid his hand with brusque familiarity on his companion's knee, and as if the hour for social and confidential greeting had only just then arrived, said: "Well, Neddy, old boy, how are you getting on?"

"So, so," said Blandford, dubiously. "You see," he began, argumentatively, "in my business there's a good deal of competition, and I was only saying this morning—"

But either Demorest was already familiar with his friend's arguments, or had as usual exhausted his topic, for without paying the slightest attention to him, he again demanded abruptly, "Why don't you go to California? Here everything's played out. That's the country for a young man like you— just starting into life, and without incumbrances. If I was free and fixed in my family affairs like you I'd go to-morrow."

There was such an occult positivism in Demorest's manner that for an instant Blandford, who had been married two years, and was transacting a steady and fairly profitable manufacturing business in the adjacent town, actually believed he was more fitted for adventurous speculation than the grimly erratic man of energetic impulses and pleasures beside him. He managed to stammer hesitatingly:

"But there's Joan—she—"

"Nonsense! Let her stay with her mother; you sell out your interest in the business, put the money into an assorted cargo, and clap it and yourself into the first ship out of Boston—and there you are. You've been married going on two years now, and a little separation until you've built up a business out there, won't do either of you any harm."

Blandford, who was very much in love with his wife, was

not, however, above putting the onus of embarrassing affection upon HER. "You don't know, Joan, Dick," he replied. "She'd never consent to a separation, even for a short time."

"Try her. She's a sensible woman—a deuced sight more than you are. You don't understand women, Ned. That's what's the matter with you."

It required all of Blandford's fond memories of his wife's conservative habits, Puritan practicality, religious domesticity, and strong family attachments, to withstand Demorest's dogmatic convictions. He smiled, however, with a certain complacency, as he also recalled the previous autumn when the first news of the California gold discovery had penetrated North Liberty, and he had expressed to her his belief that it would offer an outlet to Demorest's adventurous energy. She had received it with ill-disguised satisfaction, and the remark that if this exodus of Mammon cleared the community of the godless and unregenerate it would only be another proof of God's mysterious providence.

With the tumultuous wind at their backs it was not long before the buggy rattled once more over the cobble-stones of the town. Under the direction of his friend, Demorest, who still retained possession of the reins, drove briskly down a side street of more pretentious dwellings, where Blandford lived. One or two wayfarers looked up.

"Not so fast, Dick."

"Why? I want to bring you up to your door in style."

"Yes—but—it's Sunday. That's my house, the corner one."

They had stopped before a square, two-storied brick house,

with an equally square wooden porch supported by two plain, rigid wooden columns, and a hollow sweep of dull concavity above the door, evidently of the same architectural order as the church. There was no corner or projection to break the force of the wind that swept its smooth glacial surface; there was no indication of light or warmth behind its six closed windows.

"There seems to be nobody at home," said Demorest, briefly. "Come along with me to the hotel."

"Joan sits in the back parlor, Sundays," explained the husband.

"Shall I drive round to the barn and leave the horse and buggy there while you go in?" continued Demorest, good-humoredly, pointing to the stable gate at the side.

"No, thank you," returned Blandford, "it's locked, and I'll have to open it from the other side after I go in. The horse will stand until then. I think I'll have to say good-night, now," he added, with a sudden half-ashamed consciousness of the forbidding aspect of the house, and his own inhospitality. "I'm sorry I can't ask you in—but you understand why."

"All right," returned Demorest, stoutly, turning up his coat-collar, and unfurling his umbrella. "The hotel is only four blocks away—you'll find me there to-morrow morning if you call. But mind you tell your wife just what I told you—and no meandering of your own—you hear! She'll strike out some idea with her woman's wits, you bet. Good-night, old man!" He reached out his hand, pressed Blandford's strongly and potentially, and strode down the street.

Blandford hitched his steaming horse to a sleet-covered

horse block with a quick sigh of impatient sympathy over the animal and himself, and after fumbling in his pocket for a latchkey, opened the front door. A vista of well-ordered obscurity with shadowy trestle-like objects against the walls, and an odor of chill decorum, as if of a damp but respectable funeral, greeted him on entering. A faint light, like a cold dawn, broke through the glass pane of a door leading to the kitchen. Blandford paused in the mid-darkness and hesitated. Should he first go to his wife in the back parlor, or pass silently through the kitchen, open the back gate, and mercifully bestow his sweating beast in the stable? With the reflection that an immediate conjugal greeting, while his horse was still exposed to the fury of the blast in the street, would necessarily be curtailed and limited, he compromised by quickly passing through the kitchen into the stable yard, opening the gate, and driving horse and vehicle under the shed to await later and more thorough ministration. As he entered the back door, a faint hope that his wife might have heard him and would be waiting for him in the hall for an instant thrilled him; but he remembered it was Sunday, and that she was probably engaged in some devotional reading or exercise. He hesitatingly opened the back-parlor door with a consciousness of committing some unreasonable trespass, and entered.

She was there, sitting quietly before a large, round, shining centre-table, whose sterile emptiness was relieved only by a shaded lamp and a large black and gilt open volume. A single picture on the opposite wall—the portrait of an elderly gentleman stiffened over a corresponding volume, which he held in invincible mortmain in his rigid hand, and apparently defied posterity to take from him—seemed to offer a not uncongenial companionship. Yet the greenish light of the shade fell upon a young and pretty face, despite the color it extracted from it, and the hand that supported her low white forehead over which her full hair was simply parted, like a brown curtain, was slim and gentle-womanly. In spite of her plain lustreless silk dress, in spite of the formal frame of sombre heavy horsehair and mahogany furniture that seemed to set her off, she diffused an atmosphere of cleanly grace and prim refinement through the apartment. The priestess of this ascetic temple, the femininity of her closely covered arms, her pink ears, and a little serviceable morocco house-shoe that was visible lower down, resting on the carved lion's paw that upheld the centre-table, appeared to be only the more accented. And the precisely rounded but softly heaving bosom, that was pressed upon the edges of the open book of sermons before her, seemed to assert itself triumphantly over the rigors of the volume.

At least so her husband and lover thought, as he moved tenderly towards her. She met his first kiss on her forehead; the second, a supererogatory one, based on some supposed inefficiency in the first, fell upon a shining band of her hair, beside her neck. She reached up her slim hands, caught his wrists firmly, and, slightly putting him aside, said:

"There, Edward?"

"I drove out from Warensboro, so as to get here to-night, as I have to return to the city on Tuesday. I thought it would give me a little more time with you, Joan," he said, looking around him, and, at last, hesitatingly drawing an apparently reluctant chair from its formal position at the window. The remembrance that he had ever dared to occupy the same chair with her, now seemed hardly possible of credence.

"If it was a question of your travelling on the Lord's Day, Edward, I would rather you should have waited until to-morrow," she said, with slow precision.

"But—I—I thought I'd get here in time for the meeting," he

said, weakly.

"And instead, you have driven through the town, I suppose, where everybody will see you and talk about it. But," she added, raising her dark eyes suddenly to his, "where else have you been? The train gets into Warensboro at six, and it's only half an hour's drive from there. What have you been doing, Edward?"

It was scarcely a felicitous moment for the introduction of Demorest's name, and he would have avoided it. But he reflected that he had been seen, and he was naturally truthful. "I met Dick Demorest near the church, and as he had something to tell me, we drove down the turnpike a little way—so as to be out of the town, you know, Joan—and—and—"

He stopped. Her face had taken upon itself that appalling and exasperating calmness of very good people who never get angry, but drive others to frenzy by the simple occlusion of an adamantine veil between their own feelings and their opponents'. "I'll tell you all about it after I've put up the horse," he said hurriedly, glad to escape until the veil was lifted again. "I suppose the hired man is out."

"I should hope he was in church, Edward, but I trust YOU won't delay taking care of that poor dumb brute who has been obliged to minister to your and Mr. Demorest's Sabbath pleasures."

Blandford did not wait for a further suggestion. When the door had closed behind him, Mrs. Blandford went to the mantel-shelf, where a grimly allegorical clock cut down the hours and minutes of men with a scythe, and consulted it with a slight knitting of her pretty eyebrows. Then she fell into a vague abstraction, standing before the open book on the centre-table. Then she closed it with a snap, and methodically putting it exactly in the middle of the top of a black cabinet in the corner, lifted the shaded lamp in her hand and passed slowly with it up the stairs to her bedroom, where her light steps were heard moving to and fro. In a few moments she reappeared, stopping for a moment in the hall with the lighted lamp as if to watch and listen for her husband's return. Seen in that favorable light, her cheeks had caught a delicate color, and her dark eyes shone softly. Putting the lamp down in exactly the same place as before, she returned to the cabinet for the book, brought it again to the table, opened it at the page where she had placed her perforated cardboard book-marker, sat down beside it, and with her hands in her lap and her eyes on the page began abstractedly to tear a small piece of paper into tiny fragments. When she had reduced it to the smallest shreds, she scraped the pieces out of her silk lap and again collected them in the pink hollow of her little hand, kneeling down on the scrupulously well-swept carpet to peck up with a bird-like action of her thumb and forefinger an escaped atom here and there. These and the contents of her hand she poured into the chilly cavity of a sepulchral-looking alabaster vase that stood on the etagere. Returning to her old seat, and making a nest for her clasped fingers in the lap of her dress, she remained in that attitude, her shoulders a little narrowed and bent forward, until her husband returned.

"I've lit the fire in the bedroom for you to change your clothes by," she said, as he entered; then evading the caress which this wifely attention provoked, by bending still more primly over her book, she added, "Go at once. You're making everything quite damp here."

He returned in a few moments in his slippers and jacket, but evidently found the same difficulty in securing a conjugal and confidential contiguity to his wife. There was no apparent social centre or nucleus of comfort in the apartment; its fireplace, sealed by an iron ornament like a monumental tablet over dead ashes, had its functions superseded by an air-tight drum in the corner, warmed at second-hand from the dining-room below, and offered no attractive seclusion; the sofa against the wall was immovable and formally repellent. He was obliged to draw a chair beside the table, whose every curve seemed to facilitate his wife's easy withdrawal from side-by-side familiarity.

"Demorest has been urging me very strongly to go to California, but, of course, I spoke of you," he said, stealing his hand into his wife's lap, and possessing himself of her fingers.

Mrs. Blandford slowly lifted her fingers enclosed in his clasping hand and placed them in shameless publicity on the volume before her. This implied desecration was too much for Blandford; he withdrew his hand.

"Does that man propose to go with you?" asked Mrs. Blandford, coldly.

"No; he's preoccupied with other matters that he wanted me to talk to you about," said her husband, hesitatingly. "He is—"

"Because"—continued Mrs. Blandford in the same measured tone, "if he does not add his own evil company to his advice, it is the best he has ever given yet. I think he might have taken another day than the Lord's to talk about it, but we must not despise the means nor the hour whence the truth comes. Father wanted me to take some reasonable moment to prepare you to consider it seriously, and I thought of talking to you about it to-morrow. He thinks it would be a very judicious plan. Even Deacon Truesdail—"

"Having sold his invoice of damaged sugar kettles for mining purposes, is converted," said Blandford, goaded into momentary testiness by his wife's unexpected acquiescence and a sudden recollection of Demorest's prophecy. "You have changed your opinion, Joan, since last fall, when you couldn't bear to think of my leaving you," he added reproachfully.

"I couldn't bear to think of your joining the mob of lawless and sinful men who use that as an excuse for leaving their wives and families. As for my own feelings, Edward, I have never allowed them to stand between me and what I believed best for our home and your Christian welfare. Though I have no cause to admire the influence that I find this man, Demorest, still holds over you, I am willing to acquiesce, as you see, in what he advises for your good. You can hardly reproach ME, Edward, for worldly or selfish motives."

Blandford felt keenly the bitter truth of his wife's speech. For the moment he would gladly have exchanged it for a more illogical and selfish affection, but he reflected that he had married this religious girl for the security of an affection which he felt was not subject to the temptations of the world—or even its own weakness—as was too often the case with the giddy maidens whom he had known through Demorest's companionship. It was, therefore, more with a sense of recalling this distinctive quality of his wife than any loyalty to Demorest that he suddenly resolved to confide to her the latter's fatuous folly.

"I know it, dear," he said, apologetically, "and we'll talk it over to-morrow, and it may be possible to arrange it so that you shall go with me. But, speaking of Demorest, I think you don't quite do HIM justice. He really respects YOUR feelings and your knowledge of right and wrong more than you imagine. I actually believe he came here to-night merely to get me to interest you in an extraordinary love affair of his. I mean, Joan," he added hastily, seeing the same look of dull repression come over her face, "I mean, Joan—that is, you know, from all I can judge—it is something really serious this time. He intends to reform. And this is because he has become violently smitten with a young woman whom he has only seen half a dozen times, at long intervals, whom he first met in a railway train, and whose name and residence he don't even know."

There was an ominous silence—so hushed that the ticking of the allegorical clock came like a grim monitor. "Then," said Mrs. Blandford, in a hard, dry voice that her alarmed husband scarcely recognized, "he proposed to insult your wife by taking her into his shameful confidence."

"Good heavens! Joan, no—you don't understand. At the worst, this is some virtuous but silly school-girl, who, though she may be intending only an innocent flirtation with him, has made this man actually and deeply in love with her. Yes; it is a fact, Joan. I know Dick Demorest, and if ever there was a man honestly in love, it is he."

"Then you mean to say that this man—an utter stranger to me—a man whom I've never laid my eyes on—whom I wouldn't know if I met in the street—expects me to advise him—to—to—" She stopped. Blandford could scarcely believe his senses. There were tears in her eyes—this woman who never cried; her voice trembled—she who had always controlled her emotions.

He took advantage of this odd but opportune melting. He placed his arm around her shoulders. She tried to escape it, but with a coy, shy movement, half hysterical, half girlish, unlike her usual stony, moral precision. "Yes, Joan," he repeated, laughingly, "but whose fault is it? Not HIS, remember! And I firmly believe he thinks you can do him good."

"But he has never seen me," she continued, with a nervous little laugh, "and probably considers me some old Gorgon— like—like—Sister Jemima Skerret."

Blandford smiled with the complacency of far-reaching masculine intuition. Ah! that shrewd fellow, Demorest, was right. Joan, dear Joan, was only a woman after all.

"Then he'll be the more agreeably astonished," he returned, gayly, "and I think YOU will, too, Joan. For Dick isn't a bad-looking fellow; most women like him. It's true," he continued, much amused at the novelty of the perfectly natural toss and grimace with which Mrs. Blandford received this statement.

"I think he's been pointed out to me somewhere," she said, thoughtfully; "he's a tall, dark, dissipated-looking man."

"Nothing of the kind," laughed her husband. "He's middle-sized and as blond as your cousin Joe, only he's got a long yellow moustache, and has a quick, abrupt way of talking. He isn't at all fancy-looking; you'd take him for an energetic business man or a doctor, if you didn't know him. So you see, Joan, this correct little wife of mine has been a little, just a little, prejudiced."

He drew her again gently backwards and nearer his seat, but she caught his wrists in her slim hands, and rising from the chair at the same moment, dexterously slipped from his embrace with her back towards him. "I do not know why I should be unprejudiced by anything you've told me," she said, sharply closing the book of sermons, and, with her back still to her husband, reinstating it formally in its place on the cabinet. "It's probably one of his many scandalous pursuits of defenceless and believing women, and he, no doubt, goes off to Boston, laughing at you for thinking him in earnest; and as ready to tell his story to anybody else and boast of his double deceit." Her voice had a touch of human asperity in it now, which he had never before noticed, but recognizing, as he thought, the human cause, it was far from exciting his displeasure.

"Wrong again, Joan; he s waiting here at the Independence House for me to see him to-morrow," he returned, cheerfully. "And I believe him so much in earnest that I would be ready to swear that not another person will ever know the story but you and I and he. No, it is a real thing with him; he's dead in love, and it's your duty as a Christian to help him."

There was a moment of silence. Mrs. Blandford remained by the cabinet, methodically arranging some small articles displaced by the return of the book. "Well," she said, suddenly, "you don't tell me what mother had to say. Of course, as you came home earlier than you expected, you had time to stop THERE—only four doors from this house."

"Well, no, Joan," replied Blandford, in awkward discomfiture. "You see I met Dick first, and then—then I hurried here to you—and—and—I clean forgot it. I'm very sorry," he added, dejectedly.

"And I more deeply so," she returned, with her previous bloodless moral precision, "for she probably knows by this time, Edward, why you have omitted your usual Sabbath visit, and with WHOM you were."

"But I can pull on my boots again and run in there for a moment," he suggested, dubiously, "if you think it necessary. It won't take me a moment."

"No," she said, positively; "it is so late now that your visit would only show it to be a second thought. I will go myself—it will be a call for us both."

"But shall I go with you to the door? It is dark and sleeting," suggested Blandford, eagerly.

"No," she replied, peremptorily. "Stay where you are, and when Ezekiel and Bridget come in send them to bed, for I have made everything fast in the kitchen. Don't wait up for me."

She left the room, and in a few moments returned, wrapped from head to foot in an enormous plaid shawl. A white woollen scarf thrown over her bare brown head, and twice rolled around her neck, almost concealed her face from view. When she had parted from her husband, and reached the darkened hall below, she drew from beneath the folds of her shawl a thick blue veil, with which she completely enveloped her features. As she opened the front door and peered out into the night, her own husband would have scarcely recognized her.

With her head lowered against the keen wind she walked rapidly down the street and stopped for an instant at the door of the fourth house. Glancing quickly back at the house she had left and then at the closed windows of the one she had halted before, she gathered her skirts with one hand and sped away from both, never stopping until she reached the door of the Independence Hotel.

# CHAPTER III

Mrs. Blandford entered the side door boldly. Luckily for her, the austerities of the Sabbath were manifest even here; the bar-room was closed, and the usual loungers in the passages were absent. Without risking the recognition of her voice in an inquiry to the clerk, she slipped past the office, still muffled in her veil, and quickly mounted the narrow staircase. For an instant she hesitated before the public parlor, and glanced dubiously along the half-lit corridor. Chance befriended her; the door of a bedroom opened at that moment, and Richard Demorest, with his overcoat and hat on, stepped out in the hall.

With a quick and nervous gesture of her hand she beckoned him to approach. He came towards her leisurely, with an amused curiosity that suddenly changed to utter astonishment as she hurriedly lifted her veil, dropped it, turned, and glided down the staircase into the street again. He followed rapidly, but did not overtake her until she had reached the corner, when she slackened her pace an instant for him to join her.

"Lulu," he said eagerly; "is it you?"

"Not a word here," she said, breathlessly. "Follow me at a distance."

She started forward again in the direction of her own house. He followed her at a sufficient interval to keep her faintly distinguishable figure in sight until she had crossed three streets, and near the end of the next block glided up the steps of a house not far from the one where he remembered to have left Blandford. As he joined her, she had just succeeded in opening the door with a pass-key, and was awaiting him. With a gesture of silence she took his hand in her cold fingers, and leading him softly through the dark hall and passage, quickly entered the kitchen. Here she lit a candle, turned, and faced him. He could see that the outside shutters were bolted, and the kitchen evidently closed for the night.

As she removed the veil from her face he made a movement as if to regain her hand again, but she drew it away.

"You have forced this upon me," she said hurriedly, "and it may be ruin to us both. Why have you betrayed me?"

"Betrayed you, Lulu—Good God! what do you mean?"

She looked him full in the eye, and then said slowly, "Do you mean to say that you have told no one of our meetings?"

"Only one—my old friend Blandford, who lives—Ah, yes! I see it now. You are neighbors. He has betrayed me. This house is—"

"My father's!" she replied boldly.

The momentary uneasiness passed from Demorest's resolute face. His old self-sufficiency returned. "Good," he said, with a frank laugh, "that will do for me. Open the door there, Lulu, and take me to him. I'm not ashamed of anything I've done, my girl, nor need you be. I'll tell him my real name is Dick Demorest, as I ought to have told you before, and that I want to marry you, fairly and squarely, and let him make the conditions. I'm not a vagabond nor a thief, Lulu, if I have met you on the sly. Come, dear, let us end this now. Come—"

But she had thrown herself before him and placed her hand upon his lips. "Hush! are you mad? Listen to me, I tell you— please—oh, do—no you must not!" He had covered her hand with kisses and was drawing her face towards his own. "No—not again, it was wrong then, it is monstrous now. I implore you, listen, if you love me, stop."

He released her. She sank into a chair by the kitchen-table, and buried her flushed face in her hands.

He stood for a moment motionless before her. "Lulu, if that is your name," he said slowly, but gently, "tell me all now. Be frank with me, and trust me. If there is anything stands in the way, let me know what it is and I can overcome it. If it is my telling Ned Blandford, don't let that worry you, he's as loyal a fellow as ever breathed, and I'm a dog to ever think he willingly betrayed us. His wife, well, she's one of those pious saints—but no, she would not be such a cursed hypocrite and bigot as this."

"Hush, I tell you! WILL you hush," she said, in a frantic whisper, springing to her feet and grasping him convulsively by the lapels of his overcoat. "Not a word more, or I'll kill myself. Listen! Do you know what I brought you here for? why I left my—this house and dragged you out of your hotel? Well, it was to tell you that you must leave me, leave HERE—go out of this house and out of this town at once, to-night! And never look on it or me again! There! you have said we must end this now. It is ended, as only it could and ever would end. And if you open that door except to go, or if you attempt to—to touch me again, I'll do something desperate. There!"

She threw him off again and stepped back, strangely beautiful in the loosened shackles of her long repressed human emotion. It was as if the passion-rent robes of the priestess had laid bare the flesh of the woman dazzling and victorious. Demorest was fascinated and frightened.

"Then you do not love me?" he said with a constrained smile, "and I am a fool?"

"Love you!" she repeated. "Love you," she continued, bowing her brown head over her hanging arms and clasped hands. "What then has brought me to this? Oh," she said suddenly, again seizing him by his two arms, and holding him from her with a half-prudish, half-passionate gesture, "why could you not have left things as they were; why could we not have met in the same old way we used to meet, when I was so foolish and so happy? Why could you spoil that one dream I have clung to? Why didn't you leave me those few days of my wretched life when I was weak, silly, vain, but not the unhappy woman I am now. You were satisfied to sit beside me and talk to me then. You respected my secret, my reserve. My God! I used to think you loved me as I loved you—for THAT! Why did you break your promise and follow me here? I believed you the first day we met, when you said there was no wrong in my listening to you; that it should go no further; that you would never seek to renew it without my consent. You tell me I don't love you, and I tell you now that we must part, that frightened as I was, foolish as I was, that day was the first day I had ever lived and felt as other women live and feel. If I ran away from you then it was because I was running away from my old self too. Don't you understand me? Could you not have trusted me as I trusted you?"

"I broke my promise only when you broke yours. When you would not meet me I followed you here, because I loved you."

"And that is why you must leave me now," she said, starting from his outstretched arms again. "Do not ask me why, but go, I implore you. You must leave this town to-night, to-morrow will be too late."

He cast a hurried glance around him, as if seeking to gather some reason for this mysterious haste, or a clue for future identification. He saw only the Sabbath-sealed cupboards, the cold white china on the dresser, and the flicker of the candle on the partly-opened glass transom above the door. "As you wish," he said, with quiet sadness. "I will go now, and leave the town to-night; but"—his voice struck its old imperative note—"this shall not end here, Lulu. There will be a next time, and I am bound to win you yet, in spite of all and everything."

She looked at him with a half-frightened, half-hysterical light in her eyes. "God knows!"

"And you will be frank with me then, and tell me all?"

"Yes, yes, another time; but go now." She had extinguished the candle, turned the handle of the door noiselessly, and was holding it open. A faint light stole through the dark passage. She drew back hastily. "You have left the front door open,' she said in a frightened voice. "I thought you had shut it behind me," he returned quickly. "Good night." He drew her towards him. She resisted slightly. They were for an instant clasped in a passionate embrace; then there was a sudden collapse of the light and a dull jar. The front door had swung to.

With a desperate bound she darted into the passage and through the hall, dragging him by the hand, and threw the front door open. Without, the street was silent and empty.

"Go," she whispered frantically.

Demorest passed quickly down the steps and disappeared. At the same moment a voice came from the banisters of the landing above. "Who's there?"

"It's I, mother."

"I thought so. And it's like Edward to bring you and sneak off in that fashion."

Mrs. Blandford gave a quick sigh of relief. Demorest's flight had been mistaken for her husband's habitual evasion. Knowing that her mother would not refer to the subject again, she did not reply, but slowly mounted the dark staircase with an assumption of more than usual hesitating precaution, in order to recover her equanimity.

The clocks were striking eleven when she left her mother's house and re-entered her own. She was surprised to find a light burning in the kitchen, and Ezekiel, their hired man, awaiting her in a dominant and nasal key of religious and practical disapprobation. "Pity you wern't tu hum afore, ma'am, considerin' the doins that's goin' on in perfessed Christians' houses arter meetin' on the Sabbath Day."

"What's the difficulty now, Ezekiel?" said Mrs. Blandford, who had regained her rigorous precision once more under the decorous security of her own roof.

"Wa'al, here comes an entire stranger axin for Squire Blandford. And when I tells he warn't tu hum—"

"Not at home?" interrupted Mrs. Blandford, with a slight

start. "I left him here."

"Mebbee so, but folks nowadays don't 'pear to keer much whether they break the Sabbath or not, trapsen' raound town in and arter meetin' hours, ez if 'twor gin'ral tranin' day—and hez gone out agin."

"Go on," said Mrs. Blandford, curtly.

"Wa'al, the stranger sez, sez he, 'Show me the way to the stables,' sez he, and without taken' no for an answer, ups and meanders through the hall, outer the kitchen inter the yard, ez if he was justice of the peace; and when he gets there he sez, 'Fetch out his hoss and harness up, and be blamed quick about it, and tell Ned Blandford that Dick Demorest hez got to leave town to-night, and ez ther ain't a blamed puritanical shadbelly in this hull town ez would let a hoss go on hire Sunday night, he guesses he'll hev to borry his.' And afore I could say Jack Robinson, he tackles the hoss up and drives outer the yard, flinging this two-dollar-and-a-half-piece behind him ez if I wur a Virginia slave and he was John C. Calhoun hisself. I'd a chucked it after him if it hadn't been the Lord's Day, and it mout hev provoked disturbance."

"Mr. Demorest is worldly, but one of Edward's old friends," said Mrs. Blandford, with a slight kindling of her eyes, "and he would not have refused to aid him in what might be an errand of grace or necessity. You can keep the money, Ezekiel, as a gift, not as a wage. And go to bed. I will sit up for Mr. Blandford."

She passed out and up the staircase into her bedroom, pausing on her way to glance into the empty back parlor and take the lamp from the table. Here she noticed that her husband had evidently changed his clothes again and taken a heavier overcoat from the closet. Removing her own wraps she again descended to the lower apartment, brought out the volume of sermons, placed it and the lamp in the old position, and with her abstracted eyes on the page fell into her former attitude. Every suggestion of the passionate, half-frenzied woman in the kitchen of the house only four doors away, had vanished; one would scarcely believe she had ever stirred from the chair in which she had formally received her husband two hours before. And yet she was thinking of herself and Demorest in that kitchen.

His prompt and decisive response to her appeal, as shown in this last bold and characteristic action, relieved, while it half piqued her. But the overruling destiny which had enabled her to bring him from his hotel to her mother's house unnoticed, had protected them while there, had arrested a dangerous meeting between him and herself and her husband in her own house, impressed her more than all. It imparted to her a hideous tranquillity born of the doctrines of her youth—Predestination! She reflected with secret exultation that her moral resolution to fly from him and her conscientiously broken promise had been the direct means of bringing him there; that step by step circumstances not in themselves evil or to be combated had led her along; that even her husband and mother had felt it their duty to assist towards this fateful climax! If Edward had never kept up his worldly friendship, if she had never been restricted and compassed in her own; if she had ever known the freedom of other girls,—all this might not have happened. She had been elected to share with Demorest and her husband the effects of their ungodliness. She was no longer a free agent; what availed her resolutions? To Demorest's imperious hope, she had said, "God knows." What more could she say? Her small red lips grew white and compressed; her face rigid, her eyes hollow and abstracted; she looked like the genius of asceticism as she sat there, grimly formulating a dogmatic explanation of her lawless and unlicensed passion.

The wind had risen to a gale without, and stirred even the sealed sepulchre of the fireplace with dull rumblings and muffled moans. At times the hot-air drum in the corner seemed to expand as with some pent-up emotion. Strange currents of air crossed the empty room like the passage of unseen spirits, and she even fancied she heard whispers at the window. This caused her to rise and open it, when she found that the sleet had given way to a dry feathery snow that was swarming through the slits of the shutter; a faint reflection from the already whitened fences glimmered in the panes. She shut the window hastily, with a little shiver of cold. Where was Demorest in this storm? Would it stop him? She thought with pride now of the dominant energy that had frightened her, and knew it would not. But her husband?— what kept him? It was twelve o'clock; he had seldom stayed out so late before. During the first half hour of her reflections she had been relieved by his absence; she had even believed that he had met Demorest in the town, and was not alarmed by it, for she knew that the latter would avoid any further confidence, and cut short any return to it. But why had not Edward returned? For an instant the terrible thought that something had happened, and that they might both return together, took possession of her, and she trembled. But no; Demorest, who had already taken such extreme measures, could not consistently listen to any suggestion for delay. As her only danger lay in Demorest's presence, the absence of her husband caused her more undefinable uneasiness than actual alarm.

The room had become cold with the dying out of the dining-room fire that warmed the drum. She would go to bed. She nevertheless arranged the room again with a singular impression that she was doing it for the last time in her present existing circumstances, and placing the lamp on the table in the hall, went up to her own room. By the light of a single candle she undressed herself hastily, said her prayers punctiliously, and got into bed, with an unexpected relief at finding herself still occupying it alone. Then she fell asleep and dreamed of Demorest.

# CHAPTER IV

When Edward Blandford found himself alone after his wife had undertaken to fulfil his abandoned filial duty at her parents' house, he felt a slight twinge of self-reproach. He could not deny that this was not the first time he had evaded the sterile Sabbath evenings at his mother-in-law's, or that even at other times he was not in accord with the cold and colorless sanctity of the family. Yet he remembered that when he picked out from the budding womanhood of North Liberty this pure, scentless blossom, he had endured the privations of its surroundings with a sense of security in inhaling the atmosphere in which it grew, and knowing the integrity of its descent. There was a certain pleasure also in invading this seclusion with human passion; the first pressure of her hand when they were kneeling together at family prayers had the zest without the sin of a forbidden pleasure; the first kiss he had given her with their heads over the family Bible had fairly intoxicated him in the thin, rarefied air of their surroundings. In transplanting this blossom to his own home with the fond belief that it would eventually borrow the hues and color of his own passion, he had no further interest in the house he had left behind. When he found, however, that the ancestral influence was stronger than he expected, that the young wife, instead of assimilating to his conditions, had imported into their little household the rigors of her youthful home, he had been chilled and disappointed. But he could not help also remembering that his own boyhood had been spent in an atmosphere like her own in everything but its sincerity and deep conviction. His father had recognized the business value of placating the narrow tyranny of the respectable well-to-do religious community, and had become a conscious hypocrite and a popular citizen. He had himself been under that influence, and it was partly a conviction of this that had drawn him towards her as something genuine and real. It occurred to him now for the first time, as he looked around upon that compromise of their two lives in this chilly artificial home, that it was only natural that she would prefer the more truthful austerities of her mother's house. Had she detected the sham, and did she despise him for it?

These were questions which seemed to bring another self-accusing doubt in his own mind, although, without his being conscious of it, they had been really the outcome of that doubt. He could not help dwelling on the singular human interest she had taken in Demorest's love affair, and the utterly unexpected emotion she had shown. He had never seen her as charmingly illogical, capricious, and bewitchingly feminine. Had he not made a radical mistake in not giving her a frequent provocation for this innocent emotion —in fact, in not taking her out into a world of broader sympathies and experiences? What a household they might have had—if necessary in some other town—away from those cramped prejudices and limitations! What friends she might have been with Dick and his other worldly acquaintances; what social pleasures—guiltless amusements for her pure mind—in theatres, parties, and concerts! Would she have objected to them?—had he ever seriously proposed them to her? No! if she had objected there would have been time enough to have made this present compromise; she would have at least respected and understood his sacrifice—and his friends.

Even the artificial externals of his household had never before so visibly impressed him. Now that she was no longer in the room it did not even bear a trace of her habitation, it certainly bore no suggestion of his own. Why had he bought that hideous horsehair furniture? To remind her of the old provincial heirlooms of her father's sitting-room. Did it remind her of it? The stiff and stony emptiness of this room had been fashioned upon the decorous respectability of his own father's parlor—in which his father, who usually spent his slippered leisure in the family sitting-room, never entered except on visits from the minister. It had chilled his own youthful soul—why had he perpetuated it here?

He could only answer these questions by moodily wandering about the house, and regretting he had not gone with her. After a vain attempt to establish social and domestic relations with the hot-air drum by putting his feet upon it—after an equally futile attempt to extract interest from the book of sermons by opening its pages at random—he glanced at the clock and suddenly resolved to go and fetch her. It would remind him of the old times when he used to accompany her from church, and, after her parents had retired, spend a blissful half-hour alone with her. With what a mingling of fear and childish curiosity she used to accept his equally timid caresses! Yes, he would go and fetch her; and he would recall it to her in a whisper while they were there.

Filled with this idea, when he changed his clothes again he put on a certain heavy beaver overcoat, on whose shaggy sleeve her little, hand had so often rested when he escorted her from meeting; and he even selected the gray muffler she had knit for him in the old ante-nuptial days. It was lying in the half-opened drawer from where she had not long before taken her disguising veil.

It was still blowing in sudden, capricious gusts; and when he opened the front door the wind charged fiercely upon him, as if to drive him back. When he had finally forced his way into the street, a return current closed the door as suddenly and sharply behind him as if it had ejected him from his home for ever.

He reached the fourth house quickly, and as quickly ran up the steps; his hand was upon the bell when his eye suddenly caught sight of his wife's pass-key still in the lock. She had evidently forgotten it. Here was a chance to mischievously banter that habitually careful little woman! He slipped it into his pocket and quietly entered the dark but perfectly familiar hall. He reached the staircase without a stumble and began to ascend softly. Halfway up he heard the sound of his wife's hurried voice and another that startled him. He ascended hastily two steps, which brought him to the level of the half-opened transom of the kitchen. A candle was burning on the kitchen table; he could see everything that passed in the room; he could hear distinctly every word that was uttered.

He did not utter a cry or sound; he did not even tremble. He remained so rigid and motionless, clutching the banisters with his stiffened fingers, that when he did attempt to move, all life, as well as all that had made life possible to him, seemed to have died from him for ever. There was no nervous illusion, no dimming of his senses; he saw every-thing with a hideous clarity of perception. By some diabol-ical instantaneous photography of the brain, little actions, peculiarities, touches of gesture, expression and attitude never before noted by him in his wife, were clearly fixed and bitten in his consciousness. He saw the color of his friend's overcoat, the reddish tinge of his wife's brown hair, till then unnoticed; in that supreme moment he was aware of a sudden likeness to her mother; but more terrible than all, there seemed to be a nameless sympathetic resemblance that the guilty pair had to each other in gesture and movement as

Bret Harte

of some unhallowed relationship beyond his ken. He knew not how long he stood there without breath, without reflection, without one connected thought. He saw her suddenly put her hand on the handle of the door. He knew that in another moment they would pass almost before him. He made a convulsive effort to move, with an inward cry to God for support, and succeeded in staggering with outstretched palms against the wall, down the staircase, and blindly forward through the hall to the front door. As yet he had been able to formulate only one idea—to escape before them, for it seemed to him that their contact meant the ruin of them both, of that house, of all that was near to him—a catastrophe that struck blindly at his whole visible world. He had reached the door and opened it at the moment that the handle of the kitchen-door was turned. He mechanically fell back behind the open door that hid him, while it let the cruel light glimmer for a moment on their clasped figures. The door slipped from his nerveless fingers and swung to with a dull sound. Crouching still in the corner, he heard the quick rush of hurrying feet in the darkness, saw the door open and Demorest glide out—saw her glance hurriedly after him, close the door, and involve herself and him in the blackness of the hall. Her dress almost touched him in his corner; he could feel the near scent of her clothes, and the air stirred by her figure retreating towards the stairs; could hear the unlocking of a door above and the voice of her mother from the landing, his wife's reply, the slow fading of her footsteps on the stairs and overhead, the closing of a door, and all was quiet again. Still stooping, he groped for the handle of the door, opened it, and the next moment reeled like a drunken man down the steps into the street.

It was well for him that a fierce onset of wind and sleet at that instant caught him savagely—stirred his stagnated blood into action, and beat thought once more into his brain. He had mechanically turned towards his own home; his first effort of recovering will hurried him furiously past it and into a side street. He walked rapidly, but undeviatingly on to escape observation and secure some solitude for his returning thoughts. Almost before he knew it he was in the open fields.

The idea of vengeance had never crossed his mind. He was neither a physical nor a moral coward, but he had never felt the merely animal fury of disputed animal possession which the world has chosen to recognize as a proof of outraged sentiment, nor had North Liberty accepted the ethics that an exchange of shots equalized a transferred affection. His love had been too pure and too real to be moved like the beasts of the field, to seek in one brutal passion compensation for another. Killing—what was there to kill? All that he had to live for had been already slain. With the love that was in him—in them—already dead at his feet, what was it to him whether these two hollow lives moved on and passed him, or mingled their emptiness elsewhere? Only let them henceforth keep out of his way!

For in his first feverish flow of thought—the reaction to his benumbed will within and the beating sleet without—he believed Demorest as treacherous as his wife. He recalled his sudden and unexpected intrusion into the buggy only a few hours before, his mysterious confidences, his assurance of Joan's favorable reception of his secret, and her consent to the Californian trip. What had all this meant if not that Demorest was using him, the husband, to assist his intrigue, and carry the news of his presence in the town to her? And this boldness, this assurance, this audacity of conception was like Demorest! While only certain passages of the guilty meeting he had just seen and overheard were distinctly impressed on his mind, he remembered now, with hideous and terrible clearness, all that had gone before. It was part of the disturbed and unequal exaltation of his faculties that he

Bret Harte

dwelt more upon this and his wife's previous deceit and manifest hypocrisy, than upon the actual evidence he had witnessed of her unfaithfulness. The corroboration of the fact was stronger to him than the fact itself. He understood the coldness, the uncongeniality now—the simulated increase of her aversion to Demorest—her journeys to Boston and Hartford to see her relatives, her acquiescence to his frequent absences; not an incident, not a characteristic of her married life was inconsistent with her guilt and her deceit. He went even back to her maidenhood: how did he know this was not the legitimate sequence of other secret schoolgirl escapades The bitter worldly light that had been forced upon his simple ingenuous nature had dazzled and blinded him. He passed from fatuous credulity to equally fatuous distrust.

He stopped suddenly with the roaring of water before him. In the furious following of his rapid thought through storm and darkness he had come, he knew not how, upon the bank of the swollen river, whose endangered bridge Demorest had turned from that evening. A few steps more and he would have fallen into it. He drew nearer and looked at it with vague curiosity. Had he come there with any definite intention? The thought sobered without frightening him. There was always THAT culmination possible, and to be considered coolly.

He turned and began to retrace his steps. On his way thither he had been fighting the elements step by step; now they seemed to him to have taken possession of him and were hurrying him quickly away. But where? and to what? He was always thinking of the past. He had wandered he knew not how long, always thinking of that. It was the future he had to consider. What was to be done?

He had heard of such cases before; he had read of them in newspapers and talked of them with cold curiosity. But they were of worldly, sinful people, of dissolute men whose characters he could not conceive—of silly, vain, frivolous, and abandoned women whom he had never even met. But Joan—O God! It was the first time since his mute prayer on the staircase that the Divine name had been wrested from his lips. It came with his wife's—and his first tears! But the wind swept the one away and dried the others upon his hot cheeks.

It had ceased to rain, and the wind, which was still high, had shifted more to the north and was bitterly cold. He could feel the roadway stiffening under his feet. When he reached the pavement of the outskirts once more he was obliged to take the middle of the street, to avoid the treacherous films of ice that were beginning to glaze the sidewalks. Yet this very inclemency, added to the usual Sabbath seclusion, had left the streets deserted. He was obliged to proceed more slowly, but he met no one and could pursue his bewildering thoughts unchecked. As he passed between the lines of cold, colorless houses, from which all light and life had vanished, it seemed to him that their occupants were dead as his love, or had fled their ruined houses as he had. Why should he remain? Yet what was his duty now as a man—as a Christian? His eye fell on the hideous facade of the church he was passing—her church! He gave a bitter laugh and stumbled on again.

With one of the gusts he fancied he heard a familiar sound— the rattling of buggy wheels over the stiffening road. Or was it merely the fanciful echo of an idea that only at that moment sprung up in his mind? If it was real it came from the street parallel with the one he was in. Who could be driving out at this time? What other buggy than his own could be found to desecrate this Christian Sabbath? An irresistible thought impelled him at the risk of recognition to quicken his pace and turn the corner as Richard Demorest drove up to the Independence Hotel, sprang from his buggy, throwing the reins over the dashboard, and disappeared into the hotel!

Blandford stood still, but for an instant only. He had been wandering for an hour aimlessly, hopelessly, without consecutive idea, coherent thought or plan of action; without the faintest inspiration or suggestion of escape from his bewildering torment, without—he had begun to fear—even the power to conceive or the will to execute; when a wild idea flashed upon him with the rattle of his buggy wheels. And even as Demorest disappeared into the hotel, he had conceived his plan and executed it. He crossed the street swiftly, leaped into his buggy, lifted the reins and brought down the whip simultaneously, and the next instant was dashing down the street in the direction of the Warensboro turnpike. So sudden was the action that by the time the astonished hall porter had rushed into the street, horse and buggy had already vanished in the darkness.

Presently it began to snow. So lightly at first that it seemed a mere passing whisper to the ear, the brush of some viewless insect upon the cheek, or the soft tap of unseen fingers on the shoulders. But by the time the porter returned from his hopeless and invisible chase of the "runaway," he came in out of a swarming cloud of whirling flakes, blinded and whitened. There was a hurried consultation with the landlord, the exhibition of much imperious energy and some bank-notes from Demorest, and with a glance at the clock that marked the expiring limit of the Puritan Sabbath, the landlord at last consented. By the time the falling snow had muffled the street from the indiscreet clamor of Sabbath-breaking hoofs, the landlord's noiseless sledge was at the door and Demorest had departed.

The snow fell all that night; with fierce gusts of wind that moaned in the chimneys of North Liberty and sorely troubled the Sabbath sleep of its decorous citizens; with deep, passionless silences, none the less fateful, that softly precipitated a spotless mantle of merciful obliteration equally over their precise or their straying footprints, that would have done them good to heed and to remember; and when morning broke upon a world of week-day labor, it was covered as far as their eyes could reach as with a clear and unwritten tablet, on which they might record their lives anew. Near the wreck of the broken bridge on the Warensboro turnpike an overturned buggy lay imbedded in the drift and debris of the river hurrying silently towards the sea, and a horse with fragments of broken and icy harness still clinging to him was found standing before the stable-door of Edward Blandford. But to any further knowledge of the fate of its owner, North Liberty awoke never again.

# PART II

## CHAPTER I

The last note of the Angelus had just rung out of the crumbling fissures in the tower of the mission chapel of San Buena-ventura. The sun which had beamed that day and indeed every day for the whole dry season over the red-tiled roofs of that old and happily ventured pueblo seemed to broaden to a smile as it dipped below the horizon, as if in undiminished enjoyment of its old practical joke of suddenly plunging the Southern California coast in darkness without any preliminary twilight. The olive and fig trees at once lost their characteristic outlines in formless masses of shadow; only the twisted trunks of the old pear trees in the mission garden retained their grotesque shapes and became gruesome in the gathering gloom. The encircling pines beyond closed up their serried files; a cool breeze swept down from the coast range and, passing through them, sent their day-long heated spices through the town.

If there was any truth in the local belief that the pious incantation of the Angelus bell had the power of excluding all evil influence abroad at that perilous hour within its audible radius, and comfortably keeping all unbelieving wickedness at a distance, it was presumably ineffective as regarded the innovating stage-coach from Monterey that twice a week at that hour brought its question-asking, revolver-persuading and fortune-seeking load of passengers through the sleepy Spanish town. On the night of the 3d of August, 1856, it had not only brought but set down at the Posada one of those passengers. It was a Mr. Ezekiel Corwin, formerly known to these pages as "hired man" to the late Squire Blandford, of North Liberty, Connecticut, but now a shrewd, practical, self-sufficient, and self-asserting unit of the more cautious later Californian immigration. As the stage rattled away again with more or less humorous and open disparagement of the town and the Posada from its "outsiders," he lounged with lazy but systematic deliberation towards Mateo Morez, the proprietor.

"I guess that some of your folks here couldn't direct me to Dick Demorest's house, could ye?"

The Senor Mateo Morez was at once perplexed and pained. Pained at the ignorance thus forced upon him by a caballero; perplexed as to its intention. Between the two he smiled apologetically but gravely, and said: "No sabe, Senor. I 'ave not understood."

"No more hev I," returned Ezekiel, with patronizing recognition of his obtuseness. "I guess ez heow you ain't much on American. You folks orter learn the language if you kalkilate to keep a hotel."

But the momentary vision of a waistless woman with a shawl gathered over her head and shoulders at the back door attracted his attention. She said something to Mateo in Spanish, and the yellowish-white of Mateo's eyes glistened with intelligent comprehension.

"Ah, posiblemente; it is Don Ricardo Demorest you wish?"

Mr. Ezekiel's face and manner expressed a mingling of grateful curiosity and scme scorn at the discovery. "Wa'al," he said, looking around as if to take the entire Posada into his confidence, "way up in North Liberty, where I kem from, he was allus known as Dick Demorest, and didn't tack any forrin titles to his name. Et wouldn't hev gone down there, I reckon, 'mongst free-born Merikin citizens, no mor'n aliases would in court—and I kinder guess for the same reason. But folks get peart and sassy when they're way from hum, and put on ez many airs as a buck nigger. And so he calls hisself Don Ricardo here, does he?"

"The Senor knows Don Ricardo?" said Mateo politely.

"Ef you mean me—wa'al, yes—I should say so. He was a partiklar friend of a man I've known since he was knee-high to a grasshopper."

Ezekiel had actually never seen Demorest but once in his life. He would have scorned to lie, but strict accuracy was not essential with an ignorant foreign audience.

He took up his carpet-bag.

"I reckon I kin find his house, ef it's anyway handy."

But the Senor Mateo was again politely troubled. The house of Don Ricardo was of a truth not more than a mile distant. It was even possible that the Senor had observed it above a wall and vineyard as he came into the pueblo. But it was late—it was also dark, as the Senor would himself perceive —and there was still to-morrow. To-morrow—ah, it was always there! Meanwhile there were beds of a miraculous quality at the Posada, and a supper such as a caballero might order in his own house. Health, discretion, solicitude for oneself—all pointed clearly to to-morrow.

What part of this speech Ezekiel understood affected him only as an innkeeper's bid for custom, and as such to be steadily exposed and disposed of. With the remark that he guessed Dick Demorest's was "a good enough hotel for HIM," and that he'd better be "getting along there," he walked down the steps, carpet-bag in hand, and coolly departed, leaving Mateo pained, but smiling, on the doorstep.

"An animal with a pig's head—without doubt," said Mateo, sententiously.

"Clearly a brigand with the liver of a chicken," responded his wife.

The subject of this ambiguous criticism, happily oblivious, meantime walked doggedly back along the road the stage-coach had just brought him. It was badly paved and hollowed in the middle with the worn ruts of a century of slow undeviating ox carts, and the passage of water during the rainy season. The low adobe houses on each side, with bright cinnamon-colored tiles relieving their dark-brown walls, had the regular outlines of their doors and windows obliterated by the crumbling of years, until they looked as if they had been afterthoughts of the builder, rudely opened by pick and crowbar, and finished by the gentle auxiliary architecture of birds and squirrels. Yet these openings at times permitted glimpses of a picturesque past in the occasional view of a lace-edged pillow or silken counterpane, striped hangings, or dyed Indian rugs, the flitting of a flounced petticoat or flower-covered head, or the indolent leaning figure framed in a doorway of a man in wide velvet trousers and crimson-barred serape, whose brown face was partly hidden in a yellow nimbus of cigarette smoke. Even in the semi-darkness, Ezekiel's penetrating and impertinent eyes took eager note of these facts with superior complacency, quite unmindful, after the fashion of most critical travellers, of the hideous contrast of his own long shapeless nankeen duster, his stiff half-clerical brown straw hat, his wisp of gingham necktie, his dusty boots, his outrageous carpet-bag, and his straggling goat-like beard. A few looked at him in grave, discreet wonder. Whether they recognized in him the advent of a civilization that was destined to supplant their own ignorant, sensuous, colorful life with austere intelligence and rigid practical improvement, did not appear. He walked steadily on. As he passed the low arched door of the mission church and saw a faint light glimmering from the side windows, he had indeed a weak human desire to go in and oppose in his own person a debased and idolatrous superstition with some happily chosen question that would necessarily make the officiating priest and his congregation exceedingly uncomfortable. But he resisted; partly in the hope of meeting some idolater on his way to Benediction, and, in the guise of a stranger seeking information, dropping a few unpalatable truths; and partly because he could unbosom himself later to Demorest, who he was not unwilling to believe had embraced Popery with his adoption of a Spanish surname and title.

It had become quite dark when he reached the long wall that enclosed Demorest's premises. The wall itself excited his resentment, not only as indicating an exclusiveness highly objectionable in a man who had emigrated from a free State, but because he, Ezekiel Corwin, had difficulty in discovering the entrance. When he succeeded, he found himself before an iron gate, happily open, but savoring offensively of feudalism and tyrannical proprietorship, and passed through and entered an avenue of trees scarcely distinguishable in the darkness, whose mysterious shapes and feathery plumes were unknown to him. Numberless odors equally vague and mysterious were heavy in the air, strange and delicate plants rose dimly on either hand; enormous blossoms, like ghostly faces, seemed to peer at him from the shadows. For an instant Ezekiel succumbed to an unprofitable sense of beauty, and acquiesced in this reckless extravagance of Nature that was so unlike North Liberty. But the next moment he recovered himself, with the reflection that it was probably unhealthy, and doggedly approached the house. It was a long, one-storied, structure, apparently all roof, vine, and pillared veranda. Every window and door was open; the two or three grass hammocks swung emptily between the columns; the bamboo chairs and settees were vacant; his heavy footsteps on the floor had summoned no attendant; not even a dog had barked as he approached the house. It was shiftless, it was sinful—it boded no good to the future of Demorest.

He put down his carpet-bag on the veranda and entered the broad hall, where an old-fashioned lantern was burning on a stand. Here, too, the doors of the various apartments were open, and the rooms themselves empty of occupants. An opportunity not to be lost by Ezekiel's inquiring mind thus offered itself. He took the lantern and deliberately examined the several apartments, the furniture, the bedding, and even the small articles that were on the tables and mantels. When he had completed the round—including a corridor opening on a dark courtyard, which he did not penetrate—he returned to the hall, and set down the lantern again.

"Well," said a voice in his own familiar vernacular, "I hope you like it."

Ezekiel was surprised, but not disconcerted. What he had taken in the shadow for a bundle of serapes lying on the floor of the veranda, was the recumbent figure of a man who now raised himself to a sitting posture.

"Ez to that," drawled Ezekiel, with unshaken self-possession, "whether I like it or not ez only a question betwixt kempany

manners and truth-tellir.g. Beggars hadn't oughter be choos-
ers, and transient visitors like myself needn't allus speak their
mind. But if you mean to signify that with every door and
window open and universal shiftlessness lying round
everywhere temptin' Providence, you ain't lucky in havin' a
feller-citizen of yours drop in on ye instead of some Mexican
thief, I don't agree with ye—that's all."

The man laughed shortly and rose up. In spite of his careless
yet picturesque Mexican dress, Ezekiel instantly recognized
Demorest. With his usual instincts he was naturally pleased
to observe that he looked older and more careworn. The
softer, sensuous climate had perhaps imparted a heaviness to
his figure and a deliberation to his manner that was quite
unlike his own potential energy.

"That don't tell me who you are, and what you want," he
said, coldly.

"Wa'al then, I'm Ezekiel Corwin of North Liberty, ez used to
live with my friend and YOURS too, I guess—seein' how the
friendship was swapped into relationship—Squire Blandford."

A slight shade passed over Demorest's face. "Well," he said,
impatiently, "I don't remember you; what then?"

"You don't remember me; that's likely," returned Ezekiel
imperturbably, combing his straggling chin beard with three
fingers, "but whether it's NAT'RAL or not, considerin' the
sukumstances when we last met, ez a matter of op-pinion.
You got me to harness up the hoss and buggy the night
Squire Blandford left home, and never was heard of again.
It's true that it kem out on enquiry that the hoss and buggy
ran away from the hotel, and that you had to go out to
Warensboro in a sleigh, and the theory is that poor Squire
Blandford must have stopped the hoss and buggy

somewhere, got in and got run away agin, and pitched over the bridge. But seein' your relationship to both Squire and Mrs. Blandford, and all the sukumstances, I reckoned you'd remember it."

"I heard of it in Boston a month afterwards," said Demorest, dryly, "but I don't think I'd have recognized you. So you were the hired man who gave me the buggy. Well, I don't suppose they discharged you for it."

"No," said Ezekiel, with undisturbed equanimity. "I kalkilate Joan would have stopped that. Considerin', too, that I knew her when she was Deacon Salisbury's darter, and our fam'lies waz thick az peas. She knew me well enough when I met her in Frisco the other day."

"Have you seen Mrs. Demorest already?" said Demorest, with sudden vivacity. "Why didn't you say so before?" It was wonderful how quickly his face had lighted up with an earnestness that was not, however, without some undefinable uneasiness. The alert Ezekiel noticed it and observed that it was as totally unlike the irresistible dominance of the man of five years ago as it was different from the heavy abstraction of the man of five minutes before.

"I reckon you didn't ax me," he returned coolly. "She told me where you were, and as I had business down this way she guessed I might drop in."

"Yes, yes—it's all right, Mr. Corwin; glad you did," said Demorest, kindly but half nervously. "And you saw Mrs. Demorest? Where did you see her, and how did you think she was looking? As pretty as ever, eh?"

But the coldly literal Ezekiel was not to be beguiled into polite or ambiguous fiction. He even went to the extent of

Bret Harte

insulting deliberation before he replied. "I've seen Joan Salisbury lookin' healthier and ez far ez I kin judge doin' more credit to her stock and raisin' gin'rally," he said, thoughtfully combing his beard, "and I've seen her when she was too poor to get the silks and satins, furbelows, fineries and vanities she's flauntin' in now, and that was in Squire Blandford's time, too, I reckon. Ez to her purtiness, that's a matter of taste. You think her purty, and I guess them fellows ez was escortin' and squirin' her round Frisco thought so too, or SHE thought they did to hev allowed it."

"You are not very merciful to your townsfolk, Mr. Corwin," said Demorest, with a forced smile; "but what can I do for you?"

It was the turn for Ezekiel's face to brighten, or rather to break up, like a cold passionless mirror suddenly cracked, into various amusing but distorted reflections on the person before him. "Townies ain't to be fooled by other townies, Mr. Demorest; at least that ain't my idea o' marcy, he-he! But seen you're pressin', I don't mind tellen you MY business. I'm the only agent of Seventeen Patent Medicine Proprietors in Connecticut represented by the firm of Dilworth & Dusenberry, of San Francisco. Mebbe you heard of 'em afore—A1 druggists and importers. Wa'al, I'm openin' a field for 'em and spreadin' 'em gin'rally through these air benighted and onhealthy districts, havin' the contract for the hull State—especially for Wozun's Universal Injin Panacea ez cures everything—bein' had from a recipe given by a Sachem to Dr. Wozun's gran'ther. That bag—leavin' out a dozen paper collars and socks—is all the rest samples. That's me, Ezekiel Corwin—only agent for Californy, and that's my mission."

"Very well; but look here, Corwin," said Demorest, with a slight return of his old off-hand manner,—"I'd advise you to adopt a little more caution, and a little less criticism in your speech to the people about here, or I'm afraid you'll need the Universal Panacea for yourself. Better men than you have been shot in my presence for half your freedom."

"I guess you've just hit the bull's-eye there," replied Ezekiel, coolly, "for it's that HALF-freedom and HALF-truth that doesn't pay. I kalkilate gin'rally to speak my hull mind—and I DO. Wot's the consequence? Why, when folks find I ain't afeard to speak my mind on their affairs, they kinder guess I'm tellin' the truth about my own. Folks don't like the man that truckles to 'em, whether it's in the sellin' of a box of pills or a principle. When they re-cognize Ezekiel Corwin ain't goin' to lie about 'em to curry favor with 'em, they're ready to believe he ain't goin' to lie about Jones' Bitters or Wozun's Panacea. And, wa'al, I've been on the road just about a fortnit, and I haven't yet discovered that the original independent style introduced by Ezekiel Corwin ever broke anybody's bones or didn't pay."

And he told the truth. That remarkably unfair and unpleasant spoken man had actually frozen Hanley's Ford into icy astonishment at his audacity, and he had sold them an invoice of the Panacea before they had recovered; he had insulted Chipitas into giving an extensive order in bitters; he had left Hayward's Creek pledged to Burne's pills—with drawn revolvers still in their hands.

At another time Demorest might have been amused at his guest's audacity, or have combated it with his old imperiousness, but he only remained looking at him in a dull sort of way as if yielding to his influence. It was part of the phenomenon that the two men seemed to have changed character since they last met, and when Ezekiel said confidentially: "I reckon you're goin' to show me what room I ken stow these duds o' mine in," Demorest replied hurriedly, "Yes, certainly," and taking up his guest's carpet-bag preceded him through the hall to one of the apartments.

"I'll send Manuel to you presently," he said, putting down the bag mechanically; "the servants are not back from church, it's some saint's festival to-day."

"And so you keep a pack of lazy idolaters to leave your house to take care of itself, whilst they worship graven images," said Ezekiel, delighted at this opportunity to improve the occasion.

"If my memory isn't bad, Mr. Corwin," said Demorest dryly, "when I accompanied Mr. Blandford home the night he returned from his journey, we found YOU at church, and he had to put up his horse himself."

"But that was the Sabbath—the seventh day of the command," retorted Ezekiel.

"And here the Sabbath doesn't consist of only ONE day to serve God in," said Demorest, sententiously.

Ezekiel glanced under his white lashes at Demorest's thoughtful face. His fondest fears appeared to be confirmed; Demorest had evidently become a Papist. But that gentleman stopped any theological discussion by the abrupt inquiry:

"Did Mrs. Demorest say when she thought of returning?"

"She allowed she mout kem to-morrow—but—" added Ezekiel dubiously.

"But what?"

"Wa'al, wot with her enjyments of the vanities of this life and the kempany she keeps, I reckon she's in no hurry," said Ezekiel, cheerfully.

The entrance of Manuel here cut short any response from Demorest, who after a few directions in Spanish to the peon, left his guest to himself.

He walked to the veranda with the same dull preoccupation that Ezekiel had noticed as so different from his old decisive manner, and remained for a few moments abstractedly gazing into the dark garden. The strange and mystic shapes which had impressed even the practical Ezekiel, had become even more weird and ghost-like in the faint radiance of a rising moon.

What memories evoked by his rude guest seemed to take form and outline in that dreamy and unreal expanse!

He saw his wife again, standing as she had stood that night in her mother's house, with the white muffler around her head, and white face, imploring him to fly; he saw himself again hurrying through the driving storm to Warensboro, and reaching the train that bore him swiftly and safely miles away—that same night when her husband was perishing in the swollen river. He remembered with what strangely mingled sensations he had read the account of Blandford's death in the newspapers, and how the loss of his old friend was forgotten in the associations conjured up by his singular meeting that very night with the mysterious woman he had loved. He remembered that he had never dreamed how near and fateful were these associations; and how he had kept his promise not to seek her without her permission, until six months after, when she appointed a meeting, and revealed to him the whole truth. He could see her now, as he had seen her then, more beautiful and fascinating than ever in her black dress, and the pensive grace of refined suffering and restrained passion in her delicate face. He remembered, too, how the shock of her disclosure—the knowledge that she had been his old friend's wife—seemed only to accent her purity and suffering and his own wilful recklessness, and how it had stirred all the chivalry, generosity, and affection of his easy nature to take the whole responsibility of this innocent but compromising intrigue on his own shoulders. He had had no self-accusing sense of disloyalty to Blandford in his practical nature; he had never suspected the shy, proper girl of being his wife; he was willing to believe now, that had he known it, even that night, he would never have seen her again; he had been very foolish; he had made this poor woman participate in his folly; but he had never been dishonest or treacherous in thought or action. If Blandford had lived, even he would have admitted it. Yet he was guiltily conscious of a material satisfaction in Blandford's death, without his wife's religious conviction of the saving graces of predestination.

They had been married quietly when the two years of her widowhood had expired; his former relations with her husband and the straitened circumstances in which Blandford's death had left her having been deemed sufficient excuse in the eyes of North Liberty for her more worldly union. They had come to California at her suggestion "to begin life anew," for she had not hesitated to make this dislocation of all her antecedent surroundings as a reason as well as a condition of this marriage. She wished to see the world of which he had been a passing glimpse; to expand under his protection beyond the limits of her fettered youth. He had bought this old Spanish estate, with its near vineyard and its outlying leagues covered with wild cattle, partly from that strange contradictory predilection for peaceful husbandry common to men who have led a roving life, and partly as a check to her growing and feverish desire for change and excitement. He had at first enjoyed with an almost parental affection her childish unsophisticated delight in that world he had already wearied of, and which he had been prepared to gladly resign for her. But as the months and even years had passed without any apparent diminution in her zest for these pleasures, he tried uneasily to resume his old interest in them, and spent ten months with her in the chaotic freedom of San Francisco hotel life. But to his discomfiture he found that they no longer diverted him; to his horror he discovered that those easy gallantries in which he had spent his youth, and in which he had seen no harm, were intolerable when exhibited to his wife, and he trembled between inquietude and indignation at the copies of his former self, whom he met in hotel parlors, at theatres, and in public conveyances. The next time she visited some friends in San Francisco he did not accompany her. Though he fondly cherished his experience of her power to resist even stronger temptation, he was too practical to subject himself to the annoyance of witnessing it. In her absence he trusted her completely; his scant imagination conjured up no disturbing picture of possibilities beyond what he actually knew. In his recent questions of Ezekiel he did not expect to learn anything more. Even his guest's uncomfortable comments added no sting that he had not already felt.

With these thoughts called up by the unlooked-for advent of Ezekiel under his roof, he continued to gaze moodily into the garden. Near the house were scattered several uncouth varieties of cacti which seemed to have lost all semblance of vegetable growth, and had taken rude likeness to beasts and human figures. One high-shouldered specimen, partly hidden in the shadow, had the appearance of a man with a cloak or serape thrown over his left shoulder. As Demorest's wandering eyes at last became fixed upon it, he fancied he could trace the faint outlines of a pale face, the lower part of which was hidden by the folds of the serape. There certainly was the forehead, the curve of the dark eyebrows, the shadow of a nose, and even as he looked more steadily, a glistening of the eyes upturned to the moonlight. A sudden chill seized him. It was a horrible fancy, but it looked as might have looked the dead face of Edward Blandford! He started and ran quickly down the steps of the veranda. A slight wind at the same moment moved the long leaves and tendrils of a vine nearest him and sent a faint wave through the garden. He reached the cactus; its fantastic bulk stood plainly before him, but nothing more.

"Whar are ye runnin' to?" said the inquiring voice of Ezekiel from the veranda.

"I thought I saw some one in the garden," returned Demorest, quietly, satisfied of the illusion of his senses, "but it was a mistake."

"It mout and it moutn't," said Ezekiel, dryly. "Thar's nothin' to keep any one out. It's only a wonder that you ain't overrun with thieves and sich like."

"There are usually servants about the place," said Demorest, carelessly.

"Ef they're the same breed ez that Manuel, I reckon I'd almost as leave take my chances in the road. Ef it's all the same to you I kalkilate to put a paytent fastener to my door and winder to-night. I allus travel with them." Seeing that Demorest only shrugged his shoulders without replying, he continued, "Et ain't far from here that some folks allow is the headquarters of that cattle-stealing gang. The driver of the coach went ez far ez to say that some of these high and mighty Dons hereabouts knows more of it than they keer to tell."

"That's simply a yarn for greenhorns," said Demorest,

contemptuously. "I know all the ranch proprietors for twenty leagues around, and they've lost as many cattle and horses as I have."

"I wanter know," said Ezekiel, with grim interest. "Then you've already had consid'ble losses, eh? I kalkilate them cattle are vally'ble—about wot figger do you reckon yer out and injured?"

"Three or four thousand dollars, I suppose, altogether," replied Demorest, shortly.

"Then you don't take any stock in them yer yarns about the gang being run and protected by some first-class men in Frisco?" said Ezekiel, regretfully.

"Not much," responded Demorest, dryly; "but if people choose to believe this bluff gotten up by the petty thieves themselves to increase their importance and secure their immunity—they can. But here's Manuel to tell us supper is ready."

He led the way to the corridor and courtyard which Ezekiel had not penetrated on account of its obscurity and solitude, but which now seemed to be peopled with peons and household servants of both sexes. At the end of a long low-ceilinged room a table was spread with omelettes, chupa, cakes, chocolate, grapes, and melons, around which half a dozen attendants stood gravely in waiting. The size of the room, which to Ezekiel's eyes looked as large as the church at North Liberty, the profusion of the viands, the six attendants for the host and solitary guest, deeply impressed him. Morally rebelling against this feudal display and extravagance, he, who had disdained to even assist the Blandfords' servant-in-waiting at table and had always made his solitary meal on the kitchen dresser, was not above

Bret Harte

feeling a material satisfaction in sitting on equal terms with his master's friend and being served by these menials he despised. He did full justice to the victuals of which Demorest partook in sparing abstraction, and particularly to the fruit, which Demorest did not touch at all. Observant of his servants' eyes fixed in wonder on the strange guest who had just disposed of a second melon at supper, Demorest could not help remarking that he would lose credit as a medico with the natives unless he restrained a public exhibition of his tastes.

"Ez ha'aw?" queried Ezekiel.

"They have a proverb here that fruit is gold in the morning, silver at noon, and lead at night."

"That'll do for lazy stomicks," said the unabashed Ezekiel. "When they're once fortified by Jones' bitters and hard work, they'll be able to tackle the Lord's nat'ral gifts of the airth at any time."

Declining the cigarettes offered him by Demorest for a quid of tobacco, which he gravely took from a tin box in his pocket, and to the astonished eyes of the servants apparently obliterated any further remembrance of the meal, he accompanied his host to the veranda again, where, tilting his chair back and putting his feet on the railing, he gave himself up to unwonted and silent rumination.

The silence was broken at last by Demorest, who, half-reclining on a settee, had once or twice glanced towards the misshapen cactus.

"Was there any trace discovered of Blandford, other than we knew before we left the States?"

"Wa'al, no," said Ezekiel, thoughtfully. "The last idea was that he'd got control of the hoss after passin' the bridge, and had managed to turn him back, for there was marks of buggy wheels on the snow on the far side, and that fearin' to trust the hoss or the bridge he tried to lead him over when the bridge gave way, and he was caught in the wreck and carried off down stream. That would account for his body not bein' found; they do tell that chunks of that bridge were picked up on the Sound beach near the mouth o' the river, nigh unto sixty miles away. That's about the last idea they had of it at North Liberty." He paused and then cleverly directing a stream of tobacco juice at an accurate curve over the railing, wiped his lips with the back of his hand, and added, slowly: "Thar's another idea—but I reckon it's only mine. Leastways I ain't heard it argued by anybody."

"What is that?" asked Demorest.

"Wa'al, it ain't exakly complimentary to E. Blandford, Esq., and it mout be orkard for YOU."

"I don't think you're in the habit of letting such trifles interfere with your opinion," said Demorest, with a slightly forced laugh; "but what is your idea?"

"That thar wasn't any accident."

"No accident?" replied Demorest, raising himself on his elbow.

"Nary accident," continued Ezekiel, deliberately, "and, if it comes to that, not much of a dead body either."

"What the devil do you mean?" said Demorest, sitting up.

"I mean," said Ezekiel, with momentous deliberation, "that

E. Blandford, of the Winnipeg Mills, was in March, '50, ez nigh bein' bust up ez any man kin be without actually failin'; that he'd been down to Boston that day to get some extensions; that old Deacon Salisbury knew it, and had been pesterin' Mrs. Blandford to induce him to sell out and leave the place; and that the night he left he took about two hundred and fifty dollars in bank bills that they allus kept in the house, and Mrs. Blandford was in the habit o' hidin' in the breast-pocket of one of his old overcoats hangin' up in the closet. I mean that that air money and that air overcoat went off with him, ez Mrs. Blandford knows, for I heard her tell her ma about it. And when his affairs were wound up and his debts paid, I reckon that the two hundred and fifty was all there was left—and he scooted with it. It's orkard for you— ez I said afore—but I don't see wot on earth you need get riled for. Ef he ran off on account of only two hundred and fifty dollars he ain't goin' to run back again for the mere matter o' your marrying Joan. Ef he had—he'd a done it afore this. It's orkard ez I said—but the only orkardness is your feelin's. I reckon Joan's got used to hers."

Demorest had risen angrily to his feet. But the next moment the utter impossibility of reaching this man's hidebound moral perception by even physical force hopelessly overcame him. It would only impress him with the effect of his own disturbing power, that to Ezekiel was equal to a proof of the truth of his opinions. It might even encourage him to repeat this absurd story elsewhere with his own construction upon his reception of it. After all it was only Ezekiel's opinion—an opinion too preposterous for even a moment's serious consideration. Blandford alive, and a petty defaulter! Blandford above the earth and complacently abandoning his wife and home to another! Blandford— perhaps a sneaking, cowardly Nemesis—hiding in the shadow for future—impossible! It really was enough to make him laugh.

He did laugh, albeit with an uneasy sense that only a few years ago he would have struck down the man who had thus traduced his friend's memory.

"You've been overtaxing your brain in patent-medicine circulars, Corwin," he said in a roughly rallying manner, "and you've got rather too much highfalutin and bitters mixed with your opinions. After that yarn of yours you must be dry. What'll you take? I haven't got any New England rum, but I can give you some ten-year-old aguardiente made on the place."

As he spoke he lifted a decanter and glass from a small table which Manuel had placed in the veranda.

"I guess not," said Ezekiel dryly. "It's now goin' on five years since I've been a consistent temperance man."

"In everything but melons, and criticism of your neighbor, eh?" said Demorest, pouring out a glass of the liquor.

"I hev my convictions," said Ezekiel with affected meekness.

"And I have mine," said Demorest, tossing off the fiery liquor at a draft, "and it's that this is devilish good stuff. Sorry you can't take some. I'm afraid I'll have to get you to excuse me for a while. I have to take a ride over the ranch before turning in, to see if everything's right. The house is 'at your disposition,' as we say here. I'll see you later."

He walked away with a slight exaggeration of unconcern. Ezekiel watched him narrowly with colorless eyes beneath his white lashes. When he had gone he examined the thoroughly emptied glass of aguardiente, and, taking the decanter, sniffed critically at its sharp and potent contents. A smile of gratified discernment followed. It was clear to him that Demorest was a heavy drinker.

Contrary to his prognostication, however, Mrs. Demorest DID arrive the next day. But although he was to depart from Buenaventura by the same coach that had set her down at the gate of the casa, he had already left the house armed with some letters of introduction which Demorest had generously given him, to certain small traders in the pueblo and along the route. Demorest was not displeased to part with him before the arrival of his wife, and thus spare her the awkwardness of a repetition of Ezekiel's effrontery in her presence. Nor was he willing to have the impediment of a guest in the house to any explanation he might have to seek from her, or to the confidences that hereafter must be fuller and more mutual. For with all his deep affection for his wife, Richard Demorest unconsciously feared her. The strong man whose dominance over men and women alike had been his salient characteristic, had begun to feel an undefinable sense of some unrecognized quality in the woman he loved. He had once or twice detected it in a tone of her voice, in a remembered and perhaps even once idolized gesture, or in the accidental lapse of some bewildering word. With the generosity of a large nature he had put the thought aside, referring it to some selfish weakness of his own, or—more fatuous than all—to a possible diminution of his own affection.

He was standing on the steps ready to receive her. Few of her appreciative sex could have remained indifferent to the tender and touching significance of his silent and subdued welcome. He had that piteous wistfulness of eye seen in some dogs and the husbands of many charming women—the affection that pardons beforehand the indifference it has learned to expect. She approached him smiling in her turn, meeting the sublime patience of being unloved with the equally resigned patience of being loved, and feeling that comforting sense of virtue which might become a bore, but never a self-reproach. For the rest, she was prettier than ever; her five years of expanded life had slightly rounded the elongated oval of her face, filled up the ascetic hollows of her temples, and freed the repression of her mouth and chin. A more genial climate had quickened the circulation that North Liberty had arrested, and suffused the transparent beauty of her skin with eloquent life. It seemed as if the long, protracted northern spring of her youth had suddenly burst into a summer of womanhood under those gentle skies; and yet enough of her puritan precision of manner, movement, and gesture remained to temper her fuller and more exuberant life and give it repose. In a community of pretty women more or less given to the license and extravagance of the epoch, she always looked like a lady.

He took her in his arms and half-lifted her up the last step of the veranda. She resisted slightly with her characteristic action of catching his wrists in both her hands and holding him off with an awkward primness, and almost in the same tone that she had used to Edward Blandford five years before, said:

"There, Dick, that will do."

## CHAPTER II

Demorest's dream of a few days' conjugal seclusion and confidences with his wife was quickly dispelled by that lady. "I came down with Rosita Pico, whose father, you know, once owned this property," she said. "She's gone on to her cousins at Los Osos Rancho to-night, but comes here to-morrow for a visit. She knows the place well; in fact, she once had a romantic love affair here. But she is very entertaining. It will be a little change for us," she added, naively.

Demorest kept back a sigh, without changing his gentle smile. "I'm glad for your sake, dear. But is she not a little flighty and inclined to flirt a good deal? I think I've heard so."

"She's a young girl who has been severely tried, Richard, and perhaps is not to blame for endeavoring to forget it in such distraction as she can find," said Mrs. Demorest, with a slight return of her old manner. "I can understand her feelings perfectly." She looked pointedly at her husband as she spoke, it being one of her late habits to openly refer to their ante-nuptial acquaintance as a natural reaction from the martyr-dom of her first marriage, with a quiet indifference that seemed almost an indelicacy. But her husband only said: "As you like, dear," vaguely remembering Dona Rosita as the alleged heroine of a forgotten romance with some earlier American adventurer who had disappeared, and trying vainly to reconcile his wife's sentimental description of her with his own recollection of the buxom, pretty, laughing, but dangerous-eyed Spanish girl he had, however, seen but once.

She arrived the next day, flying into a protracted embrace of Joan, which included a smiling recognition of Demorest with an unoccupied blue eye, and a shake of her fan over his wife's shoulder. Then she drew back and seemed to take in the whole veranda and garden in another long caress of her eyes. "Ah-yess! I have recognized it, mooch. It es ze same. Of no change—not even of a leetle. No, she ess always— esso." She stopped, looked unutterable things at Joan, pressed her fan below a spray of roses on her full bodice as if to indicate some thrilling memory beneath it, shook her head again, suddenly caught sight of Demorest's serious face, said: "Ah, that brigand of our husband laughs himself at me," and then herself broke into a charming ripple of laughter.

"But I was not laughing, Dona Rosita," said Demorest, smiling sadly, however, in spite of himself.

She made a little grimace, and then raised her elbows, slightly lifting her shoulders. "As it shall please you, Senor. But he is gone—thees passion. Yess—what you shall call thees sentiment of lof—zo—as he came!" She threw her fingers in the air as if to illustrate the volatile and transitory passage of her affections, and then turned again to Joan with her back towards Demorest.

"Do please go on—Dona Rosita," said he, "I never heard the real story. If there is any romance about my house, I'd like to know it," he added with a faint sigh.

Dona Rosita wheeled upon him with an inquiring little look.

"Ah, you have the sentiment, and YOU," she continued, taking Joan by the arms, "YOU have not. Eet ess good so. When a—the wife," she continued boldly, hazarding an extended English abstraction, "he has the sentimente and the hoosband he has nothing, eet is not good—for a-him—ze wife," she concluded triumphantly.

"But I have great appreciation and I am dying to hear it," said Demorest, trying to laugh.

"Well, poor one, you look so. But you shall lif till another time," said Dona Rosita, with a mock courtesy, gliding with Joan away.

The "other time" came that evening when chocolate was served on the veranda, where Dona Rosita, mantilla-draped against the dry, clear, moonlit air, sat at the feet of Joan on the lowest step. Demorest, uneasily observant of the influence of the giddy foreigner on his wife, and conscious of certain confidences between them from which he was excluded, leaned against a pillar of the porch in half abstracted resignation; Joan, under the tutelage of Rosita, lit a cigarette; Demorest gazed at her wonderingly, trying to recall, in her fuller and more animated face, some memory of the pale, refined profile of the Puritan girl he had first met in the Boston train, the faint aurora of whose cheek in that northern clime seemed to come and go with his words. Becoming conscious at last of the eyes of Dona Rosita watching him from below, with an effort he recalled his duty as her host and gallantly reminded her that moonlight and the hour seemed expressly fitted for her promised love story.

"Do tell it," said Joan, "I don't mind hearing it again."

"Then you know it already?" said Demorest, surprised.

Joan took the cigarette from her lips, laughed complacently, and exchanged a familiar glance with Rosita. "She told it me a year ago, when we first knew each other," she replied. "Go on, dear," to Rosita.

Thus encouraged, Dona Rosita began, addressing herself first in Spanish to Demorest, who understood the language better than his wife, and lapsing into her characteristic English as she appealed to them both. It was really very little to interest Don Ricardo—this story of a silly muchacha like herself and a strange caballero. He would go to sleep while she was talking, and to-night he would say to his wife, "Mother of God! why have you brought here this chattering parrot who speaks but of one thing?" But she would go on always like the windmill, whether there was grain to grind or no. "It was four years ago. Ah! Don Ricardo did not remember the country then—it was when the first Americans came—now it is different. Then there were no coaches—in truth one travelled very little, and always on horseback, only to see one's neighbors. And suddenly, as if in one day, it was changed; there were strange men on the roads, and one was frightened, and one shut the gates of the pateo and drove the horses into the corral. One did not know much of the Americans then—for why? They were always going, going—never stopping, hurrying on to the gold mines, hurrying away from the gold mines, hurrying to look for other gold mines: but always going on foot, on horseback, in queer wagons—hurrying, pushing everywhere. Ah, it took away the breath. All, except one American—he did not hurry, he did not go with the others, he came and stayed here at Buenaventura. He was very quiet, very civil, very sad, and very discreet. He was not like the others, and always kept aloof from them. He came to see Don Andreas Pico, and wanted to beg a piece of land and an old vaquero's hut near the road for a trifle. Don Andreas would have given it, or a better house, to him, or have had him live at the casa here;

but he would not. He was very proud and shy, so he took the vaquero's hut, a mere adobe affair, and lived in it, though a caballero like yourself, with white hands that knew not labor, and small feet that had seldom walked. In good time he learned to ride like the best vaquero, and helped Don Andreas to find the lost mustangs, and showed him how to improve the old mill. And his pride and his shyness wore off, and he would come to the casa sometimes. And Don Andreas got to love him very much, and his daughter, Dona Rosita—ah, well, yes truly—a leetle.

"But he had strange moods and ways, this American, and at times they would have thought him a lunatico had they not believed it to be an American fashion. He would be very kind and gentle like one of the family, coming to the casa every day, playing with the children, advising Don Andreas and—yes—having a devotion—very discreet, very ceremonious, for Dona Rosita. And then, all in a moment, he would become as ill, without a word or gesture, until he would stalk out of the house, gallop away furiously, and for a week not be heard of. The first time it happened, Dona Rosita was piqued by his rudeness, Don Andreas was alarmed, for it was on an evening like the present, and Dona Rosita was teaching him a little song on the guitar when the fit came on him. And he snapped the guitar strings like thread and threw it down, and got up like a bear and walked away without a word."

"I see it all," said Demorest, half seriously: "you were coquetting with him, and he was jealous."

But Dona Rosita shook her head and turned impetuously, and said in English to Joan:

"No, it was astutcia—a trick, a ruse. Because when my father have arrived at his house, he is agone. And so every time. When he have the fit he goes not to his house. No. And it ees not until after one time when he comes back never again, that we have comprehend what he do at these times. And what do you think? I shall tell to you."

She composed herself comfortably, with her plump elbows on her knees, and her fan crossed on the palm of her hand before her, and began again:

"It is a year he has gone, and the stagecoach is attack of brigands. Tiburcio, our vaquero, have that night made himself a pasear on the road, and he have seen HIM. He have seen, one, two, three men came from the wood with something on the face, and HE is of them. He has nothing on his face, and Tiburcio have recognize him. We have laugh at Tiburcio. We believe him not. It is improbable that this Senor Huanson—"

"Senor who?" said Demorest.

"Huanson—eet is the name of him. Ah, Carr!—posiblemente it is nothing—a Don Fulano—or an apodo—Huanson."

"Oh, I see, JOHNSON, very likely."

"We have said it is not possible that this good man, who have come to the house and ride on his back the children, is a thief and a brigand. And one night my father have come from the Monterey in the coach, and it was stopped. And the brigands have take from the passengers the money, the rings from the finger, and the watch—and my father was of the same. And my father, he have great dissatisfaction and anguish, for his watch is given to him of an old friend, and it is not like the other watch. But the watch he go all the same. And then when the robbers have made a finish comes to the window of the coach a mascara and have say, 'Who is the Don Andreas Pico?' And my father have say, 'It is I who am Don Andreas

Pico.' And the mask have say, 'Behold, your watch is restore!' and he gif it to him. And my father say, 'To whom have I the distinguished honor to thank?' And the mask say—"

"Johnson," interrupted Demorest.

"No," said Dona Rosita in grave triumph, "he say Essmith. For this Essmith is like Huanson—an apodo—nothing."

"Then you really think this man was your old friend?" asked Demorest.

"I think."

"And that he was a robber even when living here—and that it was not your cruelty that really drove him to take the road?"

Dona Rosita shrugged her plump shoulders. "You will not comprehend. It was because of his being a brigand that he stayed not with us. My father would not have object if he have present himself to me for marriage in these times. I would not have object, for I was young, and we have knew nothing. It was he who have object. For why? Inside of his heart he have feel he was a brigand."

"But you might have reformed him in time," said Demorest.

She again shrugged her shoulders. "Quien sabe." After a pause she added with infinite gravity: "And before he have reform, it is bad for the menage. I should invite to my house some friend. They arrive, and one say, 'I have not the watch of my pocket,' and another, 'The ring of my finger, he is gone,' and another, 'My earrings, she is loss.' And I am obliged to say, 'They reside now in the pocket of my hoosband; patience! a little while—perhaps to-morrow—he will restore.' No," she continued, with an air of infinite conviction, "it is not good for the menage—the necessity of those explanation."

"You told me he was handsome," said Joan, passing her arm carelessly around Dona Rosita's comfortable waist. "How did he look?"

"As an angel! He have long curls to his back. His moustache was as silk, for he have had never a barber to his face. And his eyes—Santa Maria!—so soft and so—so melankoly. When he smile it is like the moonlight. But," she added, rising to her feet and tossing the end of her lace mantilla over her shoulder with a little laugh—"it is finish—Adelante! Dr-rrive on!"

"I don't want to destroy your belief in the connection of your friend with the road agents," said Demorest grimly, "but if he belongs to their band it is in an inferior capacity. Most of them are known to the authorities, and I have heard it even said that their leader or organizer is a very unromantic speculator in San Francisco."

But this suggestion was received coldly by the ladies, who superciliously turned their backs upon it and the suggester. Joan dropped her voice to a lower tone and turned to Dona Rosita. "And you have never seen him since?"

"Never."

"I should—at least, I wouldn't have let it end in THAT way," said Joan in a positive whisper.

"Eh?" said Dona Rosita, laughing. "So eet is YOU, Juanita, that have the romance—eh? Ah, bueno! 'you have the house—so I gif to you the lover also.' I place him at your disposition." She made a mock gesture of elaborate and complete abnegation. "But," she added in Joan's ear, with a quick glance at Demorest, "do not let our hoosband eat him. Even now he have the look to strangle ME. Make to him a little lof, quickly, when I shall walk in the garden." She turned away with a pretty wave of her fan to Demorest, and calling out, "I go to make an assignation with my memory," laughed again, and lazily passed into the shadow. An ominous silence on the veranda followed, broken finally by Mrs. Demorest.

"I don't think it was necessary for you to show your dislike to Dona Rosita quite so plainly," she said, coldly, slightly accenting the Puritan stiffness, which any conjugal tete-a-tete lately revived in her manner.

"I show dislike of Dona Rosita?" stammered Demorest, in surprise. "Come, Joan," he added, with a forgiving smile, "you don't mean to imply that I dislike her because I couldn't get up a thrilling interest in an old story I've heard from every gossip in the pueblo since I can remember."

"It's not an old story to HER," said Joan, dryly, "and even if it were, you might reflect that all people are not as anxious to forget the past as you are."

Demorest drew back to let the shaft glance by. "The story is old enough, at least for her to have had a dozen flirtations, as you know, since then," he returned gently, "and I don't think she herself seriously believes in it. But let that pass. I am sorry I offended her. I had no idea of doing so. As a rule, I think she is not so easily offended. But I shall apologize to her." He stopped and approached nearer his wife in a half-timid, half-tentative affection. "As to my forgetfulness of the past, Joan, even if it were true, I have had little cause to forget it lately. Your friend, Corwin—"

"I must insist upon your not calling him MY friend, Richard," interrupted Joan, sharply, "considering that it was through YOUR indiscretion in coming to us for the buggy that night, that he suspected—"

She stopped suddenly, for at that moment a startled little shriek, quickly subdued, rang through the garden. Demorest ran hurriedly down the steps in the direction of the outcry. Joan followed more cautiously. At the first turning of the path Dona Rosita almost fell into his arms. She was breathless and trembling, but broke into a hysterical laugh.

"I have such a fear come to me—I cry out! I think I have seen a man; but it was nothing—nothing! I am a fool. It is no one here."

"But where did you see anything?" said Joan, coming up.

Rosita flew to her side. "Where? Oh, here!—everywhere! Ah, I am a fool!" She was laughing now, albeit there were tears glistening on her lashes when she laid her head on Joan's shoulder.

"It was some fancy—some resemblance you saw in that queer cactus," said Demorest, gently. "It is quite natural, I was myself deceived the other night. But I'll look around to satisfy you. Take Dona Rosita back to the veranda, Joan. But don't be alarmed, dear—it was only an illusion."

He turned away. When his figure was lost in the entwining foliage, Dona Rosita seized Joan's shoulder and dragged her face down to a level with her own.

"It was something!" she whispered quickly.

"Who?"

Bret Harte

"It was—HIM!"

"Nonsense," groaned Joan, nevertheless casting a hurried glance around her.

"Have no fear," said Dona Rosita quickly, "he is gone—I saw him pass away—so! But it was HE—Huanson. I recognize him. I forget him never."

"Are you sure?"

"Have I the eyes? the memory? Madre de Dios! Am I a lunatico too? Look! He have stood there—so."

"Then you think he knew you were here?"

"Quien sabe?"

"And that he came here to see you?"

Dona Rosita caught her again by the shoulders, and with her lips to Joan's ear, said with the intensest and most deliberate of emphasis:

"NO!"

"What in Heaven's name brought him here then?"

"You!"

"Are you crazy?"

"You! you! YOU!" repeated Dona Rosita, with crescendo energy. "I have come upon him here; where he stood and look at the veranda, absorrrb of YOU. You move—he fly."

"Hush!"

"Ah, yes! I have said I give him to you. And he came, Bueno," murmured Dona Rosita, with a half-resigned, half-superstitious gesture.

"WILL you be quiet!"

It was the sound of Demorest's feet on the gravel path, returning from his fruitless search. He had seen nothing. It must have been Dona Rosita's fancy.

"She was just saying she thought she had been mistaken," said Joan, quietly. "Let us go in—it is rather chilly here, and I begin to feel creepy too."

Nevertheless, as they entered the house again, and the light of the hall lantern fell upon her face, Demorest thought he had never but once before seen her look so nervously and animatedly beautiful.

# CHAPTER III

The following day, when Mr. Ezekiel Corwin had delivered his letters of introduction, and thoroughly canvassed the scant mercantile community of San Buenaventura with considerable success, he deposited his carpet-bag at the stage office in the posada, and found to his chagrin that he had still two hours to wait before the coach arrived. After a vain attempt to impart cheerful but disparaging criticism of the pueblo and its people to Senor Mateo and his wife—whose external courtesy had been visibly increased by a line from Demorest, but whose confidence towards the stranger had not been extended in the same proportion—he gave it up, and threw himself lazily on a wooden bench in the veranda, already hacked with the initials of his countrymen, and drawing a jack-knife from his pocket, he began to add to that emblazonry the trade-mark of the Panacea—as a casual advertisement. During its progress, however, he was struck by the fact that while no one seemed to enter the posada through the stage office, the number of voices in the adjoining room seemed to increase, and the ministrations of Mateo and his wife became more feverishly occupied with their invisible guests. It seemed to Ezekiel that consequently there must be a second entrance which he had not seen, and this added to the circumstance that one or two lounging figures who had been approaching unaccountably disappeared before reaching the veranda, induced him to rise and examine the locality. A few paces beyond was an alley, but it appeared to be already blocked by several cigarette-smoking, short-jacketed men who were leaning against its walls, and showed no inclination to make way for him. Checked, but not daunted, Ezekiel coolly returned to the stage office, and taking the first opportunity when Mateo passed through the rear door, followed him. As he expected, the innkeeper turned to the left and entered a large room filled with tobacco smoke and the local habitues of the posada. But Ezekiel, shrewdly surmising that the private entrance must be in the opposite direction, turned to the right along the passage until he came unexpectedly upon the corridor of the usual courtyard, or patio, of every Mexican hostelry, closed at one end by a low adobe wall, in which there was a door. The free passage around the corridor was interrupted by wide partitions, fitted up with tables and benches, like stalls, opening upon the courtyard where a few stunted fig and orange trees still grew. As the courtyard seemed to be the only communication between the passage he had left and the door in the wall, he was about to cross it, when the voices of two men in the compartment struck his ears. Although one was evidently an American's, Ezekiel was instinctively convinced that they were speaking in English only for greater security against being understood by the frequenters of the posada. It is unnecessary to say that this was an innocent challenge to the curiosity of Ezekiel that he instantly accepted. He drew back carefully into the shadow of the partition as one of the voices asked—

"Wasn't that Johnson just come in?"

There was a movement as if some one had risen to look over the compartment, but the gathering twilight completely hid Ezekiel.

"No!"

"He's late. Suppose he don't come—or back out?"

The other man broke into a grim laugh. "I reckon you don't know Johnson yet, or you'd understand this yer little game o' his is just the one idea o' his life. He's been two years on that man's track, and he ain't goin' to back out now that he's got a dead sure thing on him."

"But why is he so keen about it, anyway? It don't seem nat'ral for a business man built after Johnson's style, and a rich man to boot, to go into this detective business. It ain't the reward, we know that. Is it an old grudge?"

"You bet!" The speaker paused, and then in a lower voice, which taxed Ezekial's keen ear to the uttermost, resumed: "It's said up in Frisco that Cherokee Bob knew suthin' agin Johnson way back in the States; anyhow, I believe it's understood that they came across the plains together in '50—and Bob hounded Johnson and blackmailed him here where he was livin', even to the point of makin' him help him on the road or give information, until one day Johnson bucked against it—kicked over the traces—and swore he'd be revenged on Bob, and then just settled himself down to that business. Wotever he'd been and done himself he made it all right with the sheriff here; and I've heard ez it wasn't anything criminal or that sort, but that it was o' some private trouble that he'd confided to that hound Bob, and Bob had threatened to tell agen him. That's the grudge they say Johnson has, and that's why he's allowed to be the head devil in this yer affair. It's an understood thing, too, that the sheriff and the police ain't goin' to interfere if Johnson accidentally blows the top of Bob's head off in the scrimmage of a capter."

"And I reckon Bob wouldn't hesitate to do the same thing to him when he finds out that Johnson has given him away?"

"I reckon," said the other, sententiously, "for it's Johnson's knowledge of the country and the hoss-stealers that are in with Bob's gang of road agents that made it easy for him to buy up and win over Bob's friends here, so that they'd help to trap him."

"It's pretty rough on Bob to be sold out in that way," said the second speaker, sympathizingly.

"If they were white men, p'rhaps," returned his companion, contemptuously, "but this yer's a case of Injin agen Injin, ez the men are Mexican half-breeds just as Bob's a half Cherokee. The sooner that kind o' cross cattle exterminate each other the better it'll be for the country. It takes a white man like Johnson to set 'em by the ears."

A silence followed. Ezekiel, beginning to be slightly bored with his cheaply acquired but rather impractical information, was about to slip back into the passage again when he was arrested by a laugh from the first speaker.

"What's the matter?" growled the other. "Do you want to bring the whole posada out here?"

"I was only thinkin' what a skeer them innocent greenhorn passengers will get just ez they're snoozing off for the night, ten miles from here," responded his friend, with a chuckle. "Wonder ef anybody's goin' up from here besides that patent medicine softy."

Ezekiel stopped as if petrified.

"Ef the—fools keep quiet they won't be hurt, for our men will be ready to chip in the moment of the attack. But we've got to let the attack be made for the sake of the evidence. And if we warn off the passengers from going this trip, and let the stage go up empty, Bob would suspect something and vamose. But here's Johnson!"

The door in the adobe wall had suddenly opened, and a figure in a serape entered the patio. Ezekiel, whose curiosity was whetted with indignation at the ignominious part assigned to him in this comedy, forgot even his risk of detection by the newcomer, who advanced quickly towards the compartment. When he had reached it he said, in a tone of bitterness:

"The game is up, gentlemen, and the whole thing is blown. The scoundrel has got some confederate here—for he's been seen openly on the road near Demorest's ranch, and the band have had warning and dispersed. We must find out the traitor, and take our precautions for the next time. Who is that there? I don't know him."

He was pointing to Ezekiel, who had started eagerly forward at the first sound of his voice. The two occupants of the compartment rose at the same moment, leaped into the courtyard, and confronted Ezekiel. Surrounded by the three menacing figures he did not quail, but remained intently gazing upon the newcomer. Then his mouth opened, and he drawled lazily:

"Wa'al, ef it ain't Squire Blandford, of North Liberty, Connecticut, I'm a treed coon. Squire Blandford, how DO you do?"

The stranger drew back in undisguised amazement; the two men glanced hurriedly at each other; Ezekiel alone remained cool, smiling, imperturbable, and triumphant.

"Who are YOU, sir? I do not know you," demanded the newcomer, roughly.

"Like ez not," said Corwin dryly, "it's a matter o' four year sense I lived in your house. Even Dick Demorest—you knew Dick?—didn't know me; but I reckon that Mrs. Blandford as used to be—"

"That's enough," said Blandford—for it was he—suddenly mastering both himself and Corwin by a supreme emphasis of will and gesture. "Wait!" Then turning to the two others who were discreetly regarding the blank adobe wall before them, he said: "Excuse me for a few minutes, gentlemen. There is no hurry now. I will see you later;" and with an imperative wave of his hand motioned Ezekiel to precede him into the passage, and followed him.

He did not speak until they entered the stage office, when, passing through it, he said peremptorily: "Follow me." The few loungers, who seemed to recognize him, made way for him with a singular deference that impressed Ezekiel, already dominated by his manner. The first perception in his mind was that Blandford had in some strange way succeeded to Demorest's former imperious character. There was no trace left of the old, gentle subjection to Joan's prim precision. Ezekiel followed him out of the office as unresistingly as he had followed Demorest into the stables on that eventful night. They passed down the narrow street until Blandford suddenly stopped short and turned into the crumbling doorway of one of the low adobe buildings and entered an apartment. It seemed to be the ordinary living-room of the house, made more domestic by the presence of a silk counterpaned bed in one corner, a prie Dieu and crucifix, and one or two articles of bedchamber furniture. A woman was sitting in deshabille by the window; a man was smoking on a lounge against the wall. Blandford, in the same peremptory manner, addressed a command in Spanish to the inmates, who immediately abandoned the apartment to the seeming trespasser.

Motioning his companion to a seat on the lounge just vacated, Blandford folded his arms and stood erect before him.

"Well," he said, with quick, business conciseness, "what do you want?"

Ezekiel was staggered out of his complacency.

"Wa'al," he stammered, "I only reckoned to ask the news, ez we are old friends—I—"

"How much do you want?" repeated Blandford, impatiently.

Ezekiel was mystified, yet expectant. "I can't say ez I exakly understand," he began.

"How—much—money—do—you—want," continued Blandford, with frigid accuracy, "to get up and get out of this place?"

"Wa'al, consideren ez I'm travellin' here ez the only authorized agent of a first-class Frisco Drug House," said Ezekiel, with a mingling of mortification, pride, and hopefulness, "unless you're travellin in the opposition business, I don't see what's that to you."

Blandford regarded him searchingly for an instant. "Who sent you here?"

"Dilworth & Dusenberry, Battery Street, San Francisco. Hev their card?" said Ezekiel, taking one from his waistcoat pocket.

"Corwin," said Blandford, sternly, "whatever your business is here you'll find it will pay you better, a—sight, to be frank with me and stop this Yankee shuffling. You say you have been with Demorest—what has HE got to do with your business here?"

"Nothin'," said Ezekiel. "I reckon he wos ez astonished to see me ez you are."

"And didn't he send you here to seek me?" said Blandford, impatiently.

"Considerin' he believes you a dead man, I reckon not."

Blandford gave a hard, constrained laugh. After a pause, still keeping his eyes fixed on Ezekiel, he said:

"Then your recognition of me was accidental?"

"Wa'al, yes. And ez I never took much stock in the stories that you were washed off the Warensboro Bridge, I ain't much astonished at finding you agin."

"What did you believe happened to me?" said Blandford, less brusquely.

Ezekiel noticed the softening; he felt his own turn coming. "I kalkilated you had reasons for going off, leaving no address behind you," he drawled.

"What reasons?" asked Blandford, with a sudden relapse of his former harshness.

"Wa'al, Squire Blandford, sens you wanter know—I reckon your business wasn't payin', and there was a matter of two hundred and fifty dollars ye took with ye, that your creditors would hev liked to hev back."

"Who dare say that?" demanded Blandford, angrily.

"Your wife that was—Mrs. Demorest ez is—told it to her mother," returned Ezekiel, lazily.

The blow struck deeper than even Ezekiel's dry malice imagined. For an instant, Blandford remained stupefied. In the five years' retrospect of his resolution on that fatal night, whatever doubt of its wisdom might have obtruded itself upon him, he had never thought of THIS. He had been willing to believe that his wife had quietly forgotten him as well as her treachery to him, he had passively acquiesced in the results of that forgetfulness and his own silence; he had been conscious that his wound had healed sooner than he expected, but if this consciousness had enabled him to extend a certain passive forgiveness to his wife and Demorest, it was always with the conviction that his mysterious effacement had left an inexplicable shadow upon them which their consciences alone could explain. But for this unjust, vulgar, and degrading interpretation of his own act of expiation, he was totally unprepared. It completely crushed whatever sentiment remained of that act in the horrible irony of finding himself put upon his defence before the world, without being able now to offer the real cause. The anguish of that night had gone forever; but the ridiculous interpretation of it had survived, and would survive it. In the eyes of the man before him he was not a wronged husband, but an absconding petty defaulter, whom he had just detected!

His mind was quickly made up. In that instant he had resolved upon a step as fateful as his former one, and a fitting climax to its results. For five years he had clearly misunderstood his attitude towards his treacherous wife and perjured friend. Thanks to this practical, selfish machine before him, he knew it now.

"Look here, Corwin," he said, turning upon Ezekiel a colorless face, but a steady, merciless eye. "I can guess, without your telling me, what lies may be circulated about me by the man and woman who know that I have only to declare myself alive to convict them of infamy—perhaps even of criminality before the law. You are not MY friend, or you would not have believed them; if you are THEIRS, you have two courses open to you now. Keep this meeting to yourself and trust to my mercy to keep it a secret also; or, tell Mrs. Demorest that you have seen Mr. Johnson, who is not afraid to come forward at any moment and proclaim that he is Edward Blandford, her only lawful husband. Choose which course you like—it is nothing more to me."

"Wa'al, I reckon that, as far as I know Mrs. Demorest," said Ezekiel, dryly, "it don't make the least difference to her either; but if you want to know my opinion o' this matter, it is that neither you nor Demorest exactly understand that woman. I've known Joan Salisbury since she was so high, but if ye expected me to tell you wot she was goin' to do next, I'd be able to tell ye where the next flash o' lightnin' would strike. It's wot you don't expect of Joan Salisbury that she does. And the best proof of it is that she filed papers for a divorce agin you in Chicago and got it by default a few weeks afore she married Demorest—and you don't know it."

Blandford recoiled. "Impossible," he said, but his voice too plainly showed how clearly its possibility struck him now.

"It's so, but it was kept secret by Deacon Salisbury. I overheerd it. Wa'al, that's a proof that you don't understand Joan, I reckon. And considerin' that Demorest HIMSELF don't know it, ez I found out only the other day in talking to him, I kalkilate I'm safe in sayin' that you're neither o' you quite up to Deacon Salisbury's darter in nat'ral cuteness. I don't like to obtrude my opinion, Squire Blandford, ez we're

old friends, but I do say, that wot with Demorest's prema-
tooriness and yer own hangfiredness, it's a good thing that
you two worldly men hev got Joan Salisbury to stand up for
North Liberty and keep it from bein' scandalized by the
ungodly. Ef it hadn't been for her smartness, whar y'd both
be landed now? There's a heap in Christian bringin' up, and a
power in grace, Squire Blandford."

His hard, dry face was for an instant transfigured by a grim
fealty and the dull glow of some sectarian clannishness. Or
was it possible that this woman's personality had in some
mysterious way disturbed his rooted selfishness?

During his speech Blandford had walked to the window.
When Corwin had ceased speaking, Blandford turned
towards him with an equally changed face and cold imper-
turbability that astonished him, and held out his hand. "Let
bygones be bygones, Corwin—whether we ever meet again
or not. Yet if I can do anything for you for the sake of old
times, I am ready to do it. I have some power here and in San
Francisco," he continued, with a slight touch of pride, "that
isn't dependent upon the mere name I may travel under. I
have a purpose in coming here."

"I know it," said Ezekiel, dryly. "I heard it all from your two
friends. You're huntin' some man that did you an injury."

"I'm hunting down a dog who, suspecting I had some secret
in emigrating here, tried to blackmail and ruin me," said
Blandford, with a sudden expression of hatred that seemed
inconsistent with anything that Ezekiel had ever known of
his old master's character—"a scoundrel who tried to break
up my new life as another had broken up the old." He
stopped and recovered himself with a short laugh. "Well,
Ezekiel, I don't know as his opinion of me was any worse
than yours or HERS. And until I catch HIM to clear my

name again, I let the other slanderers go."

"Wa'al, I reckon you might lay hands on that devil yet, and not far away, either. I was up at Demorest's to-day, and I heard Joan and a skittish sort o' Mexican young lady talkin' about some tramp that had frightened her. And Miss Pico said—"

"What! Who did you say?" demanded Blandford, with a violent start.

"Wa'al, I reckoned I heerd the first name too—Rosita."

A quick flush crossed Blandford's face, and left it glowing like a boy's.

"Is SHE there?"

"Wa'al, I reckon she's visitin' Joan," said Ezekiel, narrowly attentive of Blandford's strange excitement; "but wot of it?"

But Blandford had utterly forgotten Ezekiel's presence. He had remained speechless and flushed. And then, as if suddenly dazzled by an inspiration, he abruptly dashed from the room. Ezekiel heard him call to his passive host with a Spanish oath, but before he could follow, they had both hurriedly left the house.

Ezekiel glanced around him and contemplatively ran his fingers through his beard. "It ain't Joan Salisbury nor Dick Demorest ez giv' him that start! Humph! Wa'al—I wanter know!"

# CHAPTER IV

Mrs. Demorest was so fascinated by the company of Dona Rosita Pico and her romantic memories, that she prevailed upon that heart-broken but scarcely attenuated young lady to prolong her visit beyond the fortnight she had allotted to communion with the past. For a day or two following her singular experience in the garden, Mrs. Demorest plied her with questions regarding the apparition she had seen, and finally extorted from her the admission that she could not positively swear to its being the real Johnson, or even a perfectly consistent shade of that faithless man. When Joan pointed out to her that such masculine perfections as curling raven locks, long silken mustachios, and dark eyes, were attributes by no means exclusive to her lover, but were occasionally seen among other less favored and even equally dangerous Americans, Dona Rosita assented with less objection than Joan anticipated. "Besides, dear," said Joan, eying her with feline watchfulness, "it is four years since you've seen him, and surely the man has either shaved since, or else he took a ridiculous vow never to do it, and then he would be more fully bearded."

But Dona Rosita only shook her pretty head. "Ah, but he have an air—a something I know not what you call—sc." She threw her shawl over her left shoulder, and as far as a pair of soft blue eyes and comfortably pacific features would admit, endeavored to convey an idea of wicked and gloomy abstraction.

"You child," said Joan,—"that's nothing; they all of them do that. Why, there was a stranger at the Oriental Hotel whom I met twice when I was there—just as mysterious, romantic, and wicked-looking. And in fact they hinted terrible things about him. Well! so much so, that Mr. Demorest was quite foolish about my being barely civil to him—you understand —and—" She stopped suddenly, with a heightened color under the fire of Rosita's laughing eyes.

"Ah—so—Dona Discretion! Tell to me all. Did our hoosband eat him?"

Joan's features suddenly tightened to their old puritan rigidity. "Mr. Demorest has reasons—abundant reasons—to thoroughly understand and trust me," she replied in an austere voice.

Rosita looked at her a moment in mystification and then shrugged her shoulders. The conversation dropped. Nevertheless, it is worthy of being recorded that from that moment the usual familiar allusions, playful and serious, to Rosita's mysterious visitor began to diminish in frequency and finally ceased. Even the news brought by Demorest of some vague rumor in the pueblo that an intended attack on the stagecoach had been frustrated by the authorities, and that the vicinity had been haunted by incognitos of both parties, failed to revive the discussion.

Meantime the slight excitement that had stirred the sluggish life of the pueblo of San Buenaventura had subsided. The posada of Senor Mateo had lost its feverish and perplexing dual life; the alley behind it no longer was congested by lounging cigarette smokers; the compartment looking upon the silent patio was unoccupied, and its chairs and tables were empty. The two deputy sheriffs, of whom Senor Mateo presumably knew very little, had fled; and the mysterious Senor Johnson, of whom he—still presumably—knew still less, had also disappeared. For Senor Mateo's knowledge of what transpired in and about his posada, and of the character and purposes of those who frequented it, was tinctured by grave and philosophical doubts. This courteous and dignified scepticism generally took the formula of quien sabe to all frivolous and mundane inquiry. He would affirm with strict verity that his omelettes were unapproachable, his beds miraculous, his aguardiente supreme, his house was even as your own. Beyond these were questions with which the simply finite and always discreet human intellect declined to grapple.

The disturbing effect of Senor Corwin upon a mind thus gravely constituted may be easily imagined. Besides Ezekiel's inordinate capacity for useless or indiscreet information, it was undeniable that his patent medicines had effected a certain peaceful revolutionary movement in San Buenaventura. A simple and superstitious community that had steadily resisted the practical domestic and agricultural American improvements, succumbed to the occult healing influences of the Panacea and Jones's Bitters. The virtues of a mysterious balsam, more or less illuminated with a colored mythological label, deeply impressed them; and the exhibition of a circular, whereon a celestial visitant was represented as descending with a gross of Rogers' Pills to a suffering but admiring multitude, touched their religious sympathies to such an extent that the good Padre Jose was obliged to warn them from the pulpit of the diabolical character of their heresies of healing—with the natural result of yet more dangerously advertising Ezekiel. There were those too who spoke under their breath of the miraculous efficacy of these nostrums. Had not Don Victor Arguello, whose respectable digestion, exhausted by continuous pepper and garlic, failed him suddenly, received an unexpected and pleasurable stimulus from the New England rum, which was the basis of the Jones Bitters? Had not the baker, tremulous from excessive aguardiente, been soothed and sustained by the invisible morphia, judiciously hidden in Blogg's Nerve Tonic? Nor had the wily Ezekiel forgotten the weaker sex in their maiden and maternal requirements. Unguents, that made silken their black but somewhat coarsely fibrous tresses, opened charming possibilities to the Senoritas; while soothing syrups lent a peaceful repose to many a distracted mother's household. The success of Ezekiel was so marked as to justify his return at the end of three weeks with a fresh assortment and an undiminished audacity.

It was on his second visit that the sceptical, non-committal policy of Senor Mateo was sorely tried. Arriving at the posada one night, Ezekiel became aware that his host was engaged in some mysterious conference with a visitor who had entered through the ordinary public room. The view which the acute Ezekiel managed to get of the stranger, however, was productive of no further discovery than that he bore a faint and disreputable resemblance to Blandford, and was handsome after a conscious, reckless fashion, with an air of mingled bravado and conceit. But an hour later, as Corwin was taking the cooler air of the veranda before retiring to one of the miraculous beds of the posada, he was amazed at seeing what was apparently Blandford himself emerge on horseback from the alley, and after a quick glance towards the veranda, canter rapidly up the street. Ezekiel's first impression was to call to him, but the sudden recollection that he parted from his old master on confidential terms only three days before in San Francisco, and that it was impossible for him to be in the pueblo, stopped him with his fingers meditatively in his beard. Then he turned in to the posada, and hastily summoned Mateo.

The gentleman presented himself in a state of such profound scepticism that it seemed to have already communicated itself to his shoulders, and gave him the appearance of having shrugged himself into the room.

"Ha'ow long ago did Mr. Johnson get here?" asked Corwin, lazily.

"Ah—possibly—then there has been a Mr. Johnson?" This is a polite doubt of his own perceptions and a courteous acceptance of his questioner's.

"Wa'al, I guess so. Considerin' I jest saw him with my own eyes," returned Ezekiel.

"Ah!" Mateo was relieved. Might he congratulate the Senor Corwin, who must be also relieved, and shake his respected hand. Bueno. And then he had met this Senor Johnson? doubtless a friend? And he was well? and all were happy?

"Look yer, Mattayo! What I wanter know ez THIS. When did that man, who has just ridden out of your alley, come here? Sabe that—it's a plain question."

Ah surely, of the clearest comprehension. Bueno. It may have been last week—or even this week—or perhaps yesterday—or of a possibility to-day. The Senor Corwin, who was wise and omniscient, would comprehend that the difficulty lay in deciding WHO was that man. Perhaps a friend of the Senor Corwin—perhaps only one who LOOKED like him. There existed—might Mateo point out—a doubt.

Ezekiel regarded Mateo with a certain grim appreciation. "Wa'al, is there anybody here who looks like Johnson?"

Again there were the difficulty of ascertaining perfectly how the Senor Johnson looked. If the Senor Johnson was Americano, doubtless there were other Americanos who had resembled him. It was possible. The Senor Corwin had doubtless observed for a little space a caballero who was here, as it were, in the instant of the appearance of Senor Johnson? Possibly there was a resemblance, and yet—

Corwin had certainly noticed this resemblance, but it did not suit his cautious intellect to fall in with any prevailing scepticism of his host. Satisfied in his mind that Mateo was concealing something from him, and equally satisfied that he would sooner or later find it out, he grinned diabolically in the face of that worthy man, and sought the meditation of his miraculous couch. When he had departed, the sceptic turned to his wife:

"This animal has been sniffing at the trail."

"Truly—but Mother of God—where is the discretion of our friend. If he will continue to haunt the pueblo like a lovesick chicken, he will get his neck wrung yet."

Following out an ingenious idea of his own, Ezekiel called the next day on the Demorests, and in some occult fashion obtained an invitation to stay under their hospitable roof during his sojourn in Buenaventura. Perfectly aware that he owed this courtesy more to Joan than to her husband, it is probable that his grim enjoyment was not diminished by the fact; while Joan, for reasons of her own, preferred the constraint which the presence of another visitor put upon Demorest's uxoriousness. Of late, too, there were times when Dona Rosita's naive intelligence, which was not unlike the embarrassing perceptions of a bright and half-spoiled child, was in her way, and she would willingly have shared the young lady's company with her husband had Demorest shown any sympathy for the girl. It was in the faint hope that

Ezekiel might in some way beguile Rosita's wandering attention that she had invited him. The only difficulty lay in his uncouthness, and in presenting to the heiress of the Picos a man who had been formerly her own servant. Had she attempted to conceal that fact she was satisfied that Ezekiel's independence and natural predilection for embarrassing situations would have inevitably revealed it. She had even gone so far as to consider the propriety of investing him with a poor relationship to her family, when Dona Rosita herself happily stopped all further trouble. On her very first introduction to him, that charming young lady at once accepted him as a lunatic whose brains were turned by occult, scientific, and medical study! Ah! she, Rosita, had heard of such cases before. Had not a paternal ancestor of hers, one Don Diego Castro, believed he had discovered the elixir of youth. Had he not to that end refused even to wash him the hand, to cut him the nail of the finger and the hair of the head! Exalted by that discovery, had he not been unsparingly uncomplimentary to all humanity, especially to the weaker sex? Even as the Senor Corwin!

Far from being offended at this ingenious interpretation of his character, Ezekiel exhibited a dry gratification over it, and even conceived an unwholesome admiration of the fair critic; he haunted her presence and preoccupied her society far beyond Joan's most sanguine expectations. He sat in open-mouthed enjoyment of her at the table, he waylaid her in the garden, he attempted to teach her English. Dona Rosita received these extraordinary advances in a no less extra ordinary manner. In the scant masculine atmosphere of the house, and the somewhat rigid New England reserve that still pervaded it, perhaps she languished a little, and was not averse to a slight flirtation, even with a madman. Besides, she assumed the attitude of exercising a wholesome restraint over him. "If we are not found dead in our bed one morning, and extracted of our blood for a cordial, you shall thank to me for it," she said to Joan. "Also for the not empoisoning of the coffee!"

So she permitted him to carry a chair or hammock for her into the garden, to fetch the various articles which she was continually losing, and which he found with his usual penetration; and to supply her with information, in which, however, he exercised an unwonted caution. On the other hand, certain naive recollections and admissions, which in the quality of a voluble child she occasionally imparted to this "madman" in return, were in the proportion of three to one.

It had been a hot day, and even the usual sunset breeze had failed that evening to rock the tops of the outlying pine-trees or cool the heated tiles of the pueblo roofs. There was a hush and latent expectancy in the air that reacted upon the people with feverish unrest and uneasiness; even a lull in the faintly whispering garden around the Demorests' casa had affected the spirits of its inmates, causing them to wander about in vague restlessness. Joan had disappeared; Dona Rosita, under an olive-tree in one of the deserted paths, and attended by the faithful Ezekiel, had said it was "earthquake weather," and recalled, with a sign of the cross, a certain dreadful day of her childhood, when el temblor had shaken down one of the Mission towers. "You shall see it now, as he have left it so it has remain always," she added with superstitious gravity.

"That's just the lazy shiftlessness of your folks," responded Ezekiel with prompt ungallantry. "It ain't no wonder the Lord Almighty hez to stir you up now and then to keep you goin'."

Dona Rosita gazed at him with simple childish pity. "Poor man; it have affect you also in the head, this weather. So! It was even so with the uncle of my father. Hush up yourself, and bring to me the box of chocolates of my table. I will gif to you one. You shall for one time have something pleasant on the end of your tongue, even if you must swallow him after."

Ezekiel grinned. "Ye ain't afraid o' bein' left alone with the ghost that haunts the garden, Miss Rosita?"

"After YOU—never-r-r."

"I'll find Mrs. Demorest and send her to ye," said Ezekiel, hesitatingly.

"Eh, to attract here the ghost? Thank you, no, very mooch."

Ezekiel's face contracted until nothing but his bright peering gray eyes could be seen. "Attract the ghost!" he echoed. "Then you kalkilate that it's—" he stopped, insinuatingly.

Rosita brought her fan sharply over his knuckles, and immediately opened it again over her half-embarrassed face. "I comprehend not anything to 'ekalkilate.' WILL you go, Don Fantastico; or is it for me to bring to you?"

Ezekiel flew. He quickly found the chocolates and returned, but was disconcerted on arriving under the olive-tree to find Dona Rosita no longer in the hammock. He turned into a by-path, where an extraordinary circumstance attracted his attention. The air was perfectly still, but the leaves of a manzanita bush near the misshapen cactus were slightly agitated. Presently Ezekiel saw the stealthy figure of a man emerge from behind it and approach the cactus. Reaching his hand cautiously towards the plant, the stranger detached something from one of its thorns, and instantly disappeared. The quick eyes of Ezekiel had seen that it was a letter, his unerring perception of faces recognized at the same moment that the intruder was none other than the handsome, reckless-looking man he had seen the other day in conference with Mateo.

But Ezekiel was not the only witness of this strange intrusion. A few paces from him, Dona Rosita, unconscious of his return, was gazing in a half-frightened, breathless absorption in the direction of the stranger's flight.

"Wa'al!" drawled Ezekiel lazily.

She started and turned towards him. Her face was pale and alarmed, and yet to the critical eye of Ezekiel it seemed to wear an expression of gratified relief. She laughed faintly.

"Ef that's the kind o' ghost you hev about yer, it's a healthy one," drawled Ezekiel. He turned and fixed his keen eyes on Rosita's face. "I wonder what kind o' fruit grows on the cactus that he's so fond of?"

Either she had not seen the abstraction of the letter, or his acting was perfect, for she returned his look unwaveringly. "The fruit, eh? I have not comprehend."

"Wa'al, I reckon I will," said Ezekiel. He walked towards the cactus; there was nothing to be seen but its thorny spikes. He was confronted, however, by the sudden apparition of Joan from behind the manzanita at its side. She looked up and glanced from Ezekiel to Dona Rosita with an agitated air.

"Oh, you saw him too?" she said eagerly.

"I reckon," answered Ezekiel, with his eyes still on Rosita. "I was wondering what on airth he was so taken with that air cactus for."

Rosita had become slightly pale again in the presence of her friend. Joan quietly pushed Ezekiel aside and put her arm around her. "Are you frightened again?" she asked, in a low whisper.

"Not mooch," returned Rosita, without lifting her eyes.

"It was only some peon, trespassing to pick blossoms for his sweetheart," she said significantly, with a glance towards Ezekiel. "Let us go in."

She passed her hand through Rosita's passive arm and led her towards the house, Ezekiel's penetrating eyes still following Rosita with an expression of gratified doubt.

For once, however, that astute observer was wrong. When Mrs. Demorest had reached the house she slipped into her own room, and, bolting the door, drew from her bosom a letter which SHE had picked from the cactus thorn, and read it with a flushed face and eager eyes.

It may have been the effect of the phenomenal weather, but the next day a malign influence seemed to pervade the Demorest household. Dona Rosita was confined to her room by an attack of languid nerves, superinduced, as she was still voluble enough to declare, by the narcotic effect of some unknown herb which the lunatic Ezekiel had no doubt mysteriously administered to her with a view of experimenting on its properties. She even avowed that she must speedily return to Los Osos, before Ezekiel should further compromise her reputation by putting her on a colored label in place of the usual Celestial Distributer of the Panacea. Ezekiel himself, who had been singularly abstracted and reticent, and had absolutely foregone one or two opportunities of disagreeable criticism, had gone to the pueblo early that morning. The house was comparatively silent and deserted when Demorest walked into his wife's boudoir.

It was a pretty room, looking upon the garden, furnished with a singular mingling of her own inherited formal tastes and the more sensuous coloring and abandon of her new life. There were a great many rugs and hangings scattered in disorder around the room, and apparently purposeless, except for color; there was a bamboo lounge as large as a divan, with two or three cushions disposed on it, and a low chair that seemed the incarnation of indolence. Opposed to this, on the wall, was the rigid picture of her grandfather, who had apparently retired with his volume further into the canvas before the spectacle of this ungodly opulence; a large Bible on a funereal trestle-like stand, and the primmest and barest of writing-tables, before which she was standing as at a sacrificial altar. With an almost mechanical movement she closed her portfolio as her husband entered, and also shut the lid of a small box with a slight snap. This suggested exclusion of him from her previous occupation, whatever it might have been, caused a faint shadow of pain to pass across his loving eyes. He cast a glance at his wife as if mutely asking her to sit beside him, but she drew a chair to the table, and with her elbow resting on the box, resignedly awaited his speech.

"I don't mean to disturb you, darling," he said, gently, "but as we were alone, I thought we might have one of our old-fashioned talks, and—"

"Don't let it be so old-fashioned as to include North Liberty again," she interrupted, wearily. "We've had quite enough of that since I returned."

"I thought you found fault with me then for forgetting the past. But let that pass, dear; it is not OUR affairs I wanted to talk to you about now," he said, stifling a sigh, "it's about your friend. Please don't misunderstand what I am going to say; nor that I interpose except from necessity."

She turned her dark brown eyes in his direction, but her glance passed abstractedly over his head into the garden.

"It's a matter perfectly well known to me—and, I fear, to all our servants also—that somebody is making clandestine visits to our garden. I would not trouble you before, until I ascertained the object of these visits. It is quite plain to me now that Dona Rosita is that object, and that communications are secretly carried on between her and some unknown stranger. He has been here once or twice before; he was here again yesterday. Ezekiel saw him and saw her."

"Together?" asked Mrs. Demorest, sharply.

"No; but it was evident that there was some understanding, and that some communication passed between them."

"Well?" said Mrs. Demorest, with repressed impatience.

"It is equally evident, Joan, that this stranger is a man who does not dare to approach your friend in her own house, nor more openly in this; but who, with her connivance, uses us to carry on an intrigue which may be perfectly innocent, but is certainly compromising to all concerned. I am quite willing to believe that Dona Rosita is only romantic and reckless, but that will not prevent her from becoming a dupe of some rascal who dare not face us openly, and who certainly does not act as her equal."

"Well, Rosita is no chicken, and you are not her guardian."

There was a vague heartlessness, more in her voice than in her words, that touched him as her cold indifference to himself had never done, and for an instant stung his crushed spirit to revolt. "No" he said, sternly, "but I am her father's FRIEND, and I shall not allow his daughter to be compromised under my roof."

Her eyes sprang up to meet his in hatred as promptly as they once had met in love. "And since when, Richard Demorest, have you become so particular?" she began, with dry asperity. "Since you lured ME from the side of my wedded husband? Since you met ME clandestinely in trains and made love to ME under an assumed name? Since you followed ME to my house under the pretext of being my husband's friend, and forced me—yes, forced me—to see you secretly under my mother's roof? Did you think of compromising ME then? Did you think of ruining my reputation, of driving my husband from his home in despair? Did you call yourself a rascal then? Did you—"

"Stop!" he said, in a voice that shook the rafters; "I command you, stop!"

She had gradually worked herself from a deliberately insulting precision into an hysterical, and it is to be feared a virtuous, conviction of her wrongs. Beginning only with the instinct to taunt and wound the man before her, she had been led by a secret consciousness of something else he did not know to anticipate his reproach and justify herself in a wild feminine abandonment of emotion. But she stopped at his words. For a moment she was even thrilled again by the strength and imperiousness she had loved.

They were facing each other after five years of mistaken passion, even as they had faced each other that night in her mother's kitchen. But the grave of that dead passion yawned between them. It was Joan who broke the silence, that after her single outburst seemed to fill and oppress the room.

"As far as Rosita is concerned," she said, with affected calmness, "she is going to-night. And you probably will not be troubled any longer by your mysterious visitor."

Whether he heeded the sarcastic significance of her last sentence, or even heard her at all, he did not reply. For a moment he turned his blazing eyes full upon her, and then without a word strode from the room.

She walked to the door and stood uneasily listening in the passage until she heard the clatter of hoofs in the paved patio, and knew that he had ordered his horse. Then she turned back relieved to her room.

It was already sunset when Demorest drew rein again at the entrance of the corral, and the last stroke of the Angelus was ringing from the Mission tower. He looked haggard and exhausted, and his horse was flecked with foam and dirt. Wherever he had been, or for what object, or whether, objectless and dazed, he had simply sought to lose himself in aimlessly wandering over the dry yellow hills or in careering furiously among his own wild cattle on the arid, brittle plain; whether he had beaten all thought from his brain with the jarring leap of his horse, or whether he had pursued some vague and elusive determination to his own door, is not essential to this brief chronicle. Enough that when he dismounted he drew a pistol from his holster and replaced it in his pocket.

He had just pushed open the gate of the corral as he led in his horse by the bridle, when he noticed another horse tethered among some cotton woods that shaded the outer wall of his garden. As he gazed, the figure of a man swung lightly from one of the upper boughs of a cotton-wood on the wall and disappeared on the other side. It was evidently the clandestine visitor. Demorest was in no mood for trifling. Hurriedly driving his horse into the enclosure with a sharp cut of his riata, he closed the gate upon him, slipped past the intervening space into the patio, and then unnoticed into the upper part of the garden. Taking a narrow by-path in the direction of the cotton woods that could be seen above the wall, he presently came in sight of the object of his search moving stealthily towards the house. It was the work of a moment only to dash forward and seize him, to find himself engaged in a sharp wrestle, to half draw his pistol as he struggled with his captive in the open. But once in the clearer light, he started, his grasp of the stranger relaxed, and he fell back in bewildered terror.

"Edward Blandford! Good God!"

The pistol had dropped from his hand as he leaned breathless against a tree. The stranger kicked the weapon contemptuously aside. Then quietly adjusting his disordered dress, and picking the brambles from his sleeve, he said with the same air of disdain, "Yes! Edward Blandford, whom you thought dead! There! I'm not a ghost—though you tried to make me one this time," he said, pointing to the pistol.

Demorest passed his hand across his white face. "Then it's you—and you have come here for—for—Joan?"

"For Joan?" echoed Blandford, with a quick scornful laugh, that made the blood flow back into Demorest's face as from a blow, and recalled his scattered senses. "For Joan," he repeated. "Not much!"

The two men were facing each other in irreconcilable yet confused antagonism. Both were still excited and combative from their late physical struggle, but with feelings so widely different that it would have been impossible for either to have comprehended the other. In the figure that had apparently risen from the dead to confront him, Demorest only saw the man he had unconsciously wronged—the man who had it in his power to claim Joan and exact a terrible retribution! But it was part of this monstrous and irreconcilable situation that Blandford had ceased to contemplate it, and in his preoccupation only saw the actual interference of a man whom he no longer hated, but had begun to pity and despise.

He glanced coolly around him. "Whatever we've got to say to each other," he said deliberately, "had better not be overheard. At least what I have got to say to you."

# CHAPTER V

Demorest, now as self-possessed as his adversary, haughtily waved his hand towards the path. They walked on in silence, without even looking at each other, until they reached a small summer-house that stood in the angle of the wall. Demorest entered. "We cannot be heard here," he said curtly.

"And we can see what is going on. Good," said Blandford, coolly following him. The summer-house contained a bench and a table. Blandford seated himself on the bench. Demorest remained standing beside the table. There was a moment's silence.

"I came here with no desire to see you or avoid you," said Blandford, with cold indifference. "A few weeks ago I might perhaps have avoided you, for your own sake. But since then I have learned that among the many things I owe to—to your wife is the fact that five years ago she secretly DIVORCED ME, and that consequently my living presence could neither be a danger nor a menace to you. I see," he added, dryly, with a quick glance at Demorest's horror-stricken face, "that I was also told the truth when they said you were as ignorant of the divorce as I was."

He stopped, half in pity of his adversary's shame, half in surprise of his own calmness. Five years before, in the

Bret Harte

tumultuous consciousness of his wrongs, he would have scarcely trusted himself face to face with the cooler and more self-controlled Demorest. He wondered at and partly admired his own coolness now, in the presence of his enemy's confusion.

"As your mind is at rest on that point," he continued, sarcastically, "I don't suppose you care to know what became of ME when I left North Liberty. But as it happens to have something to do with my being here to-night, and is a part of my business with you, you'll have to listen to it. Sit down! Very well, then—stand up! It's your own house."

His half cynical, wholly contemptuous ignoring of the real issue between them was more crushing to Demorest than the keenest reproach or most tragic outburst. He did not lift his eyes as Blandford resumed in a dry, business-like way:

"When I came across the plains to California, I fell in with a man about my own age—an emigrant also. I suppose I looked and acted like a crazy fool through all the journey, for he satisfied himself that I had some secret reason for leaving the States, and suspected that I was, like himself—a criminal. I afterwards learned that he was an escaped thief and assassin. Well, he played upon me all the way here, for I didn't care to reveal my real trouble to him, lest it should get back to North liberty—" He interrupted himself with a sarcastic laugh. "Of course, you understand that all this while Joan was getting her divorce unknown to me, and you were marrying her—yet as I didn't know anything about it I let him compromise me to save her. But"—he stopped, his eye kindled, and, losing his self-control in what to Demorest seemed some incoherent passion, went on excitedly: "that man continued his persecution HERE—yes, HERE, in this very house, where I was a trusted and honored guest, and threatened to expose me to a pure, innocent, simple girl who had taken pity on me—unless I helped him in a conspiracy of cattle-stealers and road agents, of which he was chief. I was such a cursed sentimental fool then, that believing him capable of doing this, believing myself still the husband of that woman, your wife, and to spare that innocent girl the shame of thinking me a villain, I purchased his silence by consenting. May God curse me for it!"

He had started to his feet with flashing eyes, and the indication of an overmastering passion that to Demorest, absorbed only in the stupefying revelation of his wife's divorce and the horrible doubt it implied, seemed utterly vacant and unmeaning.

He had often dreamed of Blandford as standing before him, reproachful, indignant, and even desperate over his wife's unfaithfulness; but this insane folly and fury over some trivial wrong done to that plump, baby-faced, flirting Dona Rosita, crushed him by its unconscious but degrading obliteration of Joan and himself more than the most violent denunciation. Dazed and bewildered, yet with the instinct of a helpless man, he clung only to that part of Blandford's story which indicated that he had come there for Rosita, and not to separate him from Joan, and even turned to his former friend with a half-embarrassed gesture of apology as he stammered—

"Then it was YOU who were Rosita's lover, and you who have been here to see her. Forgive me, Ned—if I had only known it." He stopped and timidly extended his hand. But Blandford put it aside with a cold gesture and folded his arms.

"You have forgotten all you ever knew of me, Demorest! I am not in the habit of making clandestine appointments with helpless women whose natural protectors I dare not face. I have never pursued an innocent girl to the house I dared not enter. When I found that I could not honorably retain Dona Rosita's affection, I fled her roof. When I believed that even if I broke with this scoundrel—as I did—I was still legally if not morally tied to your wife, and could not marry Rosita, I left her never to return. And I tore my heart out to do it."

The tears were standing in his eyes. Demorest regarded him again with vacant wonder. Tears!—not for Joan's unfaithfulness to him—but for this silly girl's transitory sentimentalism. It was horrible!

And yet what was Joan to Blandford now? Why should he weep for the woman who had never loved him—whom he loved no longer? The woman who had deceived him—who had deceived them BOTH. Yes! for Joan must have suspected that Blandford was living to have sought her secret divorce—and yet she had never told him—him—the man for whom she got it. Ah! he must not forget THAT! It was to marry him that she had taken that step. It was perhaps a foolish caution—a mistaken reservation; but it was the folly—the mistake of a loving woman. He hugged this belief the closer, albeit he was conscious at the same time of following Blandford's story of his alienated affection with a feeling of wonder and envy.

"And what was the result of this touching sacrifice?" continued Blandford, trying to resume his former cynical indifference. "I'll tell you. This scoundrel set himself about to supplant me. Taking advantage of my absence, his knowledge that her affection for me was heightened by the mystery of my life, and trusting to profit by a personal resemblance he is said to bear to me, he began to haunt her. Lately he has grown bolder, and he dared even to communicate with her here. For it is he," he continued, again giving way to his passion, "this dog, this sneaking coward, who visits the place unknown to you, and thinks to entrap the poor girl through her memory of me. And it is he that I came here to prevent, to expose—if necessary to kill! Don't misunderstand me. I have made myself a deputy of the law for that purpose. I've a warrant in my pocket, and I shall take him, this mongrel, half-breed Cherokee Bob, by fair means or foul!"

The energy and presence of his passion was so infectious that it momentarily swept away Demorest's doubts of the past. "And I will help you, before God, Blandford," he said eagerly. "And Joan shall, too. She will find out from Rosita how far—"

"Thank you," interrupted Blandford, dryly; "but your wife has already interfered in this matter, to my cost. It is to her, I believe, I owe this wretch's following Rosita here. She already knows this man—has met him twice in San Francisco; he even boasts of YOUR jealousy. You know best how far he lied."

But Demorest had braced himself against the chill sensation that had begun to creep over him as Blandford spoke. He nerved himself and said, proudly, "I forbade her knowing him on account of his reputation solely. I have no reason to believe she has ever even wished to disobey me."

A smile of scorn that had kindled in Blandford's eyes, darkened with a swift shadow of compassion as he glanced at Demorest's hard, ashen face. He held out his hand with a sudden impulse. "Enough, I accept your offer, and shall put it to the test this very night. I know—if you do not—that Rosita is to leave here for Los Osos an hour from now in a private carriage, which your wife has ordered especially for her. The same information tells me that this villain and another of his gang will be in wait for the carriage three miles out of the pueblo to attack it and carry off the young girl."

"Are you mad!" said Demorest, in unfeigned amazement. "Do you believe them capable of attacking a private carriage and carrying off a solitary, defenceless woman? Come, Blandford, this is a school-girl romance—not an act of mercenary highwaymen—least of all Cherokee Bob and his gang. This is some madness of Rosita's, surely," he continued with a forced laugh.

"Does this mean that you think better of your promise?" asked Blandford, dryly.

"I said I was at your service," said Demorest, reproachfully.

"Then hear my plan to prevent it, and yet take that dog in the act," said Blandford. "But we must first wait here till the last moment to ascertain if he makes any signal to show that his plan is altered, or that he has discovered he is watched." He turned, and in his preoccupation laid his hand for an instant upon Demorest's shoulder with the absent familiarity of old days. Unconscious as the action was, it thrilled them both— from its very unconsciousness—and impelled them to throw themselves into the new alliance with such feverish and excited activity in order to preclude any dangerous alien reflection, that when they rose a few moments later and cautiously left the garden arm-in-arm through the outer gates, no one would have believed they had ever been estranged, least of all the clever woman who had separated them.

It was nearly nine o'clock when the two friends, accompanied by the sheriff of the county, left San Buenaventura turnpike and turned into a thicket of alders to wait the coming of the carriage they were to henceforth follow cautiously and unseen in a parallel trail to the main road. The moon had risen, and with it the long withheld wind that now swept over the distant stretch of gleaming road and partly veiled it at times with flying dust unchecked by any dew from the clear cold sky. Demorest shivered even with his ready hand on his revolver. Suddenly the sheriff uttered an exclamation of disgust.

"Blasted if thar ain't some one in the road between us and their ambush."

"It's one of their gang—scouting. Lie close."

"Scout be darned. Look at him bucking round there in the dust. He can't even ride! It's some blasted greenhorn taking a pasear on a hoss for the first time. Damnation! he's ruined everything. They'll take the alarm."

"I'll push on and clear him out," said Blandford, excitedly. "Even if they're off, I may yet get a shot at the Cherokee."

"Quick then," said Demorest, "for here comes the carriage." He pointed to a dark spot on the road occasionally emerging from the driven dust clouds.

In another moment Blandford was at the heels of the awkward horseman, who wheeled clumsily at his approach and revealed the lank figure of Ezekiel Corwin!

"You here!" said Blandford, in stupefied fury.

"Wa'al, yes, squire," said Ezekiel lazily, in spite of his uneasy seat. "I kalkilated ef there was suthin' goin' on, I'd like to see it."

"You cursed prying fool! you've spoiled all. There!" he

shouted despairingly, as the quick clatter of hoofs rang from the arroyo behind them, "there they go! That's your work, blockhead! Out of my way, or by God—" but the sentence was left unfinished as, joined by the sheriff, who had galloped up at the sound of the robbers' flight, he darted past the unconcerned Ezekiel. Demorest would have followed, but Blandford, with a warning cry to him to remain and protect the carriage, halted him at the side of Corwin as the vehicle now rapidly approached.

But Ezekiel was before him even then, and as the driver pulled up, that inquiring man tumbled from his horse, ran to the door and opened it. Demorest rode up, glanced into the carriage, and fell back in blank amazement.

It was his wife who was sitting there alone, pale, erect, and beautiful. By some illusion of the moonlight, her face and figure, covered with soft white wrappings for a journey, looked as he remembered to have seen her the first night they had met in the Boston train. The picture was completed by the traveling bag and rug that lay on the seat before her. Another terrible foreboding seized him; his brain reeled. Was he going mad?

"Joan!" he stammered. "You? What is the meaning of this?"

Ezekiel whom but for his dazed condition he might have seen violently contorting his features in Joan's face, presumably in equal astonishment—broke into a series of discordant chuckles.

"Wa'al, ef that ain't Deacon Salisbury's darter all over. Ha! Here are ye two men folks makin' no end o' fuss to save that Mexican gal with pistols and ambushes and plots and counterplots, and yer's Joan Salisbury shows ye the way ha'ow to do it. And so, ma'am, you succeeded in fixin' it up with Dona Rosita to take her place and just sell them robbers cheap! Wa'al, ma'am, yer sold this yer party, too—for"—he advanced his face close to hers—"I never let on a word, though I knew it, and although they nearly knocked me off my hoss in their fuss and fury. Ha! ha! They wanted to know what I was doin' here, he-he! Tell 'em, Joan, tell 'em."

Demorest gazed from one to another with a troubled face, yet one on which a faint relief was breaking.

"What does he mean, Joan? Speak," he said, almost imploringly.

Joan, whose color was slightly returning, drew herself up with her old cold Puritan precision.

"After the scene you made this morning, Richard, when you chose to accuse your wife of unfaithfulness to her friend, her guest, and even your reputation, I resolved to go myself with Dona Rosita to Los Osos and explain the matter to her father. Some rumor of the ridiculous farce I have just witnessed reached us through Ezekiel, and frightened the poor girl so that she declined—and properly, too to face the hoax which you and some nameless impersonator of a disgraced fugitive have gotten up for purposes of your own! I wish you joy of your work! If the play is over now, I presume I may be allowed to proceed on my journey?"

"Not yet," said Demorest slowly, with a face over which the chasing doubts had at last settled in a grayish pallor. "Believe what you like, misunderstand me if you will, laugh at the danger you perhaps comprehend better than I do, but upon this road, wherever or to whatever it was leading you—to-night you go no further!"

"Then I suppose I may return home," she said coldly.

"Ezekiel will accompany me back to protect me from— robbers. Come, Ezekiel. Mr. Demorest and his friends can be safely trusted to take care of—your horse."

And as the grinning Ezekiel sprang into the carriage beside her, she pulled up the glass in the fateful and set face of her once trusting husband; the carriage turned and drove off, leaving him like a statue in the road.

*****

The bell of the North Liberty Second Presbyterian Church had just ceased ringing. But in the last five years it had rung out the bass viol and harmonium, and rung in an organ and choir; and the old austere interior had been subjected at the hands of the rising generation to an invasion of youthful warmth and color. Nowhere was this more apparent than in the choir itself, where the bright spring sunshine, piercing a newly-opened stained-glass window, picked out the new spring bonnet of Mrs. Demorest and settled upon it during the singing of the hymn. Perhaps that was the reason why a few eyes were curiously directed in that direction, and that even the minister himself strayed from the precise path of doctrine to allude with ecclesiastical vagueness to certain shining examples of the Christian virtues that were "again in our midst." The shrewd face and white eyelashes of Ezekiel Corwin, junior partner in the firm of Dilworth & Dusenberry, of San Francisco, were momentarily raised towards the choir, and then relapsed into an expression of fatigued self-righteousness.

When the service was over a few worshipers lingered near the choir staircase, mindful of the spring bonnet.

"It looks quite nat'ral," said Deacon Fairchild, "ter see Joan Salisbury attendin' the ministration of the Word agin. And I ain't sorry she didn't bring that second husband of hers with her. It kinder looks like old times—afore Edward Blandford was gathered to the Lord."

"That's so," replied his auditor meekly, "and they do say ez ha'ow Demorest got more powerful worldly and unregenerate in that heathen country, and that Joan ez a professin' Christian had to leave him. I've heerd tell thet he'd got mixed up, out thar, with some half-breed outlaw, of the name o' Johnson, ez hez a purty, high-flyin' Mexican wife. It was fort'nit for Joan that she found a friend in grace in Brother Corwin to look arter her share in the property and bring her back tu hum."

"She's lookin' peart," said Sister Bradley, "though to my mind that bonnet savors still o' heathen vanities."

"Et's the new idees—crept in with that organ," groaned Deacon Fairchild; "but—sho—thar she comes."

She shone for an instant—a charming vision—out of the shadow of the choir stairs, and then glided primly into the street.

The old sexton, still in waiting with his hand on the half-closed door, paused and looked after her with a troubled brow. A singular and utterly incomprehensible recollection and resemblance had just crossed his mind.

# ABOUT THE AUTHOR

**Francis Bret Harte** (August 25, 1836–May 6, 1902) was an American author and poet, best remembered for his accounts of pioneering life in California.

Born in Albany, New York, Harte moved to California in 1853, later working there in a number of capacities, including miner, teacher, messenger, and journalist. He spent part of his life in the northern California coast town now known as Arcata, at the time it was just a mining camp on Humboldt Bay.

His first literary efforts, including poetry and prose, appeared in The Californian, an early literary journal edited by Charles Henry Webb. In 1868 he became editor of The Overland Monthly, another new literary magazine, but this one more in tune with the pioneering spirit of excitement in California. His story, "The Luck of Roaring Camp," appeared in the magazine's second edition, propelling Harte to nationwide fame.

As an established literary figure, he was appointed to the position of United States Consul in the town of Krefeld, Germany in 1878 and Glasgow in 1880. In 1885 he settled in London. During the thirty years he spent in Europe, he never abandoned writing, and maintained a prodigious output of stories that retained the freshness of his earlier work. He died in England in 1902.

# Choose from Thousands of 1stWorldLibrary Classics By

A. M. Barnard
Ada Leverson
Adolphus William Ward
Aesop
Agatha Christie
Alexander Aaronsohn
Alexander Kielland
Alexandre Dumas
Alfred Gatty
Alfred Ollivant
Alice Duer Miller
Alice Turner Curtis
Alice Dunbar
Allen Chapman
Alleyne Ireland
Ambrose Bierce
Amelia E. Barr
Amory H. Bradford
Andrew Lang
Andrew McFarland Davis
Andy Adams
Angela Brazil
Anna Alice Chapin
Anna Sewell
Annie Besant
Annie Hamilton Donnell
Annie Payson Call
Annie Roe Carr
Annonaymous
Anton Chekhov
Archibald Lee Fletcher
Arnold Bennett
Arthur C. Benson
Arthur Conan Doyle
Arthur M. Winfield
Arthur Ransome
Arthur Schnitzler
Arthur Train
Atticus
B.H. Baden-Powell
B. M. Bower
B. C. Chatterjee
Baroness Emmuska Orczy
Baroness Orczy
Basil King
Bayard Taylor
Ben Macomber
Bertha Muzzy Bower
Bjornstjerne Bjornson

Booth Tarkington
Boyd Cable
Bram Stoker
C. Collodi
C. E. Orr
C. M. Ingleby
Carolyn Wells
Catherine Parr Traill
Charles A. Eastman
Charles Amory Beach
Charles Dickens
Charles Dudley Warner
Charles Farrar Browne
Charles Ives
Charles Kingsley
Charles Klein
Charles Hanson Towne
Charles Lathrop Pack
Charles Romyn Dake
Charles Whibley
Charles Willing Beale
Charlotte M. Braeme
Charlotte M. Yonge
Charlotte Perkins Stetson
Clair W. Hayes
Clarence Day Jr.
Clarence E. Mulford
Clemence Housman
Confucius
Coningsby Dawson
Cornelis DeWitt Wilcox
Cyril Burleigh
D. H. Lawrence
Daniel Defoe
David Garnett
Dinah Craik
Don Carlos Janes
Donald Keyhoe
Dorothy Kilner
Dougan Clark
Douglas Fairbanks
E. Nesbit
E. P. Roe
E. Phillips Oppenheim
E. S. Brooks
Earl Barnes
Edgar Rice Burroughs
Edith Van Dyne
Edith Wharton

Edward Everett Hale
Edward J. O'Biren
Edward S. Ellis
Edwin L. Arnold
Eleanor Atkins
Eleanor Hallowell Abbott
Eliot Gregory
Elizabeth Gaskell
Elizabeth McCracken
Elizabeth Von Arnim
Ellem Key
Emerson Hough
Emilie F. Carlen
Emily Bronte
Emily Dickinson
Enid Bagnold
Enilor Macartney Lane
Erasmus W. Jones
Ernie Howard Pie
Ethel May Dell
Ethel Turner
Ethel Watts Mumford
Eugene Sue
Eugenie Foa
Eugene Wood
Eustace Hale Ball
Evelyn Everett-green
Everard Cotes
F. H. Cheley
F. J. Cross
F. Marion Crawford
Fannie E. Newberry
Federick Austin Ogg
Ferdinand Ossendowski
Fergus Hume
Florence A. Kilpatrick
Fremont B. Deering
Francis Bacon
Francis Darwin
Frances Hodgson Burnett
Frances Parkinson Keyes
Frank Gee Patchin
Frank Harris
Frank Jewett Mather
Frank L. Packard
Frank V. Webster
Frederic Stewart Isham
Frederick Trevor Hill
Frederick Winslow Taylor

Friedrich Kerst
Friedrich Nietzsche
Fyodor Dostoyevsky
G.A. Henty
G.K. Chesterton
Gabrielle E. Jackson
Garrett P. Serviss
Gaston Leroux
George A. Warren
George Ade
Geroge Bernard Shaw
George Cary Eggleston
George Durston
George Ebers
George Eliot
George Gissing
George MacDonald
George Meredith
George Orwell
George Sylvester Viereck
George Tucker
George W. Cable
George Wharton James
Gertrude Atherton
Gordon Casserly
Grace E. King
Grace Gallatin
Grace Greenwood
Grant Allen
Guillermo A. Sherwell
Gulielma Zollinger
Gustav Flaubert
H. A. Cody
H. B. Irving
H.C. Bailey
H. G. Wells
H. H. Munro
H. Irving Hancock
H. R. Naylor
H. Rider Haggard
H. W. C. Davis
Haldeman Julius
Hall Caine
Hamilton Wright Mabie
Hans Christian Andersen
Harold Avery
Harold McGrath
Harriet Beecher Stowe
Harry Castlemon
Harry Coghill
Harry Houidini

Hayden Carruth
Helent Hunt Jackson
Helen Nicolay
Hendrik Conscience
Hendy David Thoreau
Henri Barbusse
Henrik Ibsen
Henry Adams
Henry Ford
Henry Frost
Henry James
Henry Jones Ford
Henry Seton Merriman
Henry W Longfellow
Herbert A. Giles
Herbert Carter
Herbert N. Casson
Herman Hesse
Hildegard G. Frey
Homer
Honore De Balzac
Horace B. Day
Horace Walpole
Horatio Alger Jr.
Howard Pyle
Howard R. Garis
Hugh Lofting
Hugh Walpole
Humphry Ward
Ian Maclaren
Inez Haynes Gillmore
Irving Bacheller
Isabel Cecilia Williams
Isabel Hornibrook
Israel Abrahams
Ivan Turgenev
J.G.Austin
J. Henri Fabre
J. M. Barrie
J. M. Walsh
J. Macdonald Oxley
J. R. Miller
J. S. Fletcher
J. S. Knowles
J. Storer Clouston
J. W. Duffield
Jack London
Jacob Abbott
James Allen
James Andrews
James Baldwin

James Branch Cabell
James DeMille
James Joyce
James Lane Allen
James Lane Allen
James Oliver Curwood
James Oppenheim
James Otis
James R. Driscoll
Jane Abbott
Jane Austen
Jane L. Stewart
Janet Aldridge
Jens Peter Jacobsen
Jerome K. Jerome
Jessie Graham Flower
John Buchan
John Burroughs
John Cournos
John F. Kennedy
John Gay
John Glasworthy
John Habberton
John Joy Bell
John Kendrick Bangs
John Milton
John Philip Sousa
John Taintor Foote
Jonas Lauritz Idemil Lie
Jonathan Swift
Joseph A. Altsheler
Joseph Carey
Joseph Conrad
Joseph E. Badger Jr
Joseph Hergesheimer
Joseph Jacobs
Jules Vernes
Julian Hawthrone
Julie A Lippmann
Justin Huntly McCarthy
Kakuzo Okakura
Karle Wilson Baker
Kate Chopin
Kenneth Grahame
Kenneth McGaffey
Kate Langley Bosher
Kate Langley Bosher
Katherine Cecil Thurston
Katherine Stokes
L. A. Abbot
L. T. Meade

L. Frank Baum
Latta Griswold
Laura Dent Crane
Laura Lee Hope
Laurence Housman
Lawrence Beasley
Leo Tolstoy
Leonid Andreyev
Lewis Carroll
Lewis Sperry Chafer
Lilian Bell
Lloyd Osbourne
Louis Hughes
Louis Joseph Vance
Louis Tracy
Louisa May Alcott
Lucy Fitch Perkins
Lucy Maud Montgomery
Luther Benson
Lydia Miller Middleton
Lyndon Orr
M. Corvus
M. H. Adams
Margaret E. Sangster
Margret Howth
Margaret Vandercook
Margaret W. Hungerford
Margret Penrose
Maria Edgeworth
Maria Thompson Daviess
Mariano Azuela
Marion Polk Angellotti
Mark Overton
Mark Twain
Mary Austin
Mary Catherine Crowley
Mary Cole
Mary Hastings Bradley
Mary Roberts Rinehart
Mary Rowlandson
M. Wollstonecraft Shelley
Maud Lindsay
Max Beerbohm
Myra Kelly
Nathaniel Hawthrone
Nicolo Machiavelli
O. F. Walton
Oscar Wilde

Owen Johnson
P.G. Wodehouse
Paul and Mabel Thorne
Paul G. Tomlinson
Paul Severing
Percy Brebner
Percy Keese Fitzhugh
Peter B. Kyne
Plato
Quincy Allen
R. Derby Holmes
R. L. Stevenson
R. S. Ball
Rabindranath Tagore
Rahul Alvares
Ralph Bonehill
Ralph Henry Barbour
Ralph Victor
Ralph Waldo Emmerson
Rene Descartes
Ray Cummings
Rex Beach
Rex E. Beach
Richard Harding Davis
Richard Jefferies
Richard Le Gallienne
Robert Barr
Robert Frost
Robert Gordon Anderson
Robert L. Drake
Robert Lansing
Robert Lynd
Robert Michael Ballantyne
Robert W. Chambers
Rosa Nouchette Carey
Rudyard Kipling
Saint Augustine
Samuel B. Allison
Samuel Hopkins Adams
Sarah Bernhardt
Sarah C. Hallowell
Selma Lagerlof
Sherwood Anderson
Sigmund Freud
Standish O'Grady
Stanley Weyman
Stella Benson
Stella M. Francis

Stephen Crane
Stewart Edward White
Stijn Streuvels
Swami Abhedananda
Swami Parmananda
T. S. Ackland
T. S. Arthur
The Princess Der Ling
Thomas A. Janvier
Thomas A Kempis
Thomas Anderton
Thomas Bailey Aldrich
Thomas Bulfinch
Thomas De Quincey
Thomas Dixon
Thomas H. Huxley
Thomas Hardy
Thomas More
Thornton W. Burgess
U. S. Grant
Upton Sinclair
Valentine Williams
Various Authors
Vaughan Kester
Victor Appleton
Victor G. Durham
Victoria Cross
Virginia Woolf
Wadsworth Camp
Walter Camp
Walter Scott
Washington Irving
Wilbur Lawton
Wilkie Collins
Willa Cather
Willard F. Baker
William Dean Howells
William le Queux
W. Makepeace Thackeray
William W. Walter
William Shakespeare
Winston Churchill
Yei Theodora Ozaki
Yogi Ramacharaka
Young E. Allison
Zane Grey